MW01479842

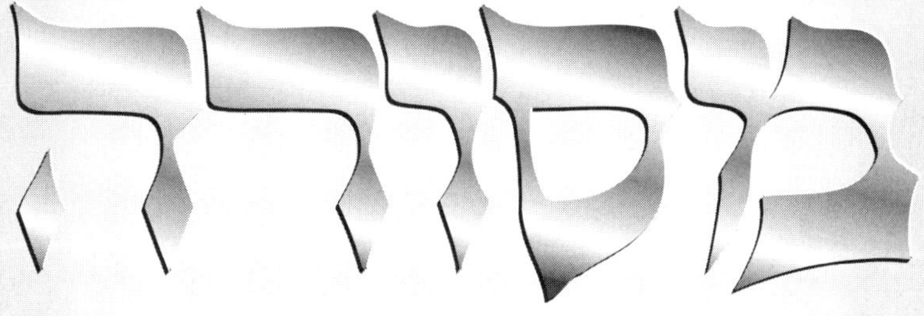

ArtScroll Series

Rabbi Nosson Scherman / Rabbi Meir Zlotowitz

General Editors

WITH ALL

Published by
Mesorah Publications, ltd

YOUR HEART

Heart-warming stories of devotion and inspiration

RABBI BINYOMIN PRUZANSKY

FIRST EDITION
First Impression ... August 2012

Published and Distributed by
MESORAH PUBLICATIONS, LTD.
4401 Second Avenue / Brooklyn, N.Y 11232

Distributed in Europe by
LEHMANNS
Unit E, Viking Business Park
Rolling Mill Road
Jarow, Tyne & Wear, NE32 3DP
England

Distributed in Israel by
SIFRIATI / A. GITLER — BOOKS
6 Hayarkon Street
Bnei Brak 51127

Distributed in Australia and New Zealand
by **GOLDS WORLDS OF JUDAICA**
3-13 William Street
Balaclava, Melbourne 3183
Victoria, Australia

Distributed in South Africa by
KOLLEL BOOKSHOP
Northfield Centre, 17 Northfield Avenue
Glenhazel 2192, Johannesburg, South Africa

ARTSCROLL SERIES
WITH ALL YOUR HEART
© *Copyright 2012, by* MESORAH PUBLICATIONS, Ltd.
4401 Second Avenue / Brooklyn, N.Y. 11232 / (718) 921-9000 / www.artscroll.com

ALL RIGHTS RESERVED
The text, prefatory and associated textual contents and introductions — including the typographic layout, cover artwork and ornamental graphics — have been designed, edited and revised as to content, form and style.

No part of this book may be reproduced IN ANY FORM, PHOTOCOPYING, OR COMPUTER RETRIEVAL SYSTEMS — even for personal use without written permission from the copyright holder, Mesorah Publications Ltd.
except by a reviewer who wishes to quote brief passages in connection with a review written for inclusion in magazines or newspapers.

THE RIGHTS OF THE COPYRIGHT HOLDER WILL BE STRICTLY ENFORCED.

To contact the author for speaking engagements or comments, he can be reached via e-mail at bpruz@yeshivanet.com

ISBN 10: 1-4226-1301-1 / ISBN 13: 978-1-4226-1301-6

Typography by CompuScribe at ArtScroll Studios, Ltd.

Printed in the United States of America by Noble Book Press Corp.
Bound by Sefercraft, Quality Bookbinders, Ltd., Brooklyn N.Y. 11232

הרב דוד קוויאט

ר"מ בישיבת מיר

ורב דאגודת ישראל סניף חפץ חיים

בס"ד בין המצרים תשס"ז

לכבוד תלמידי ידידי יקירי הרב ר' בנימין יהודה פרוזאנסקי שליט"א. שכתב ספר ושמו הוא "Stories For The Jewish Heart".

והוא נכתב לעורר הלב היהודי לעבודת ה' יתברך. וזהו כשמו כן הוא, שמלהיב הלבבות לאביהם שבשמים, שמעשה של קידוש השם ומעשה חסדים של עבדי ה' הם מעוררים את האדם שגם כן הוא בעצמו יכול לעשות כזה מכח הכוחות הטובים מה שיש בהאדם עצמו בכל יהודי ויהודי בפנימיותו מכח אבותיו הקדושים. ואל יאמר האדם שאין זה עבורי, רק שיש בכוח שלו שיעשה נמי דוגמתו.

ואכן ספרו הראשון כבר פעל בו גדולות, ואברכהו שיצליח בספרו השנית להגדיל תורה ולהאדירה, כחפצו הטהורה ויפוצו מעינותיו חוצה לברכה ולהצלחה.

ממני ידידו, ומכירו שהשקפותיו הם בדרך התורה והיראה, ומברכו באהבת נפשי בכל לב.

דוד קויאט

דוד קויאט

Michtav Berachah from Rabbi Dovid Kviat זצ"ל for *Stories for the Jewish Heart*

Table of Contents

Author's Preface

We say it three times a day: "*V'ahavta eis Hashem Elokecha* ***bechal levavcha*** — and you shall love Hashem, your G-d, **with all your heart**." Did you ever wonder why the Torah says, "with *all* your heart"? Why is it not enough to love Hashem with your heart?

I believe that the word "all" teaches us that in fulfilling the commandment to love Hashem, mediocrity will not do. Rather, we have to love Him with every fiber of our being. Because Hashem is purely and completely devoted to our good and welfare, like a father to his young child, we must reciprocate in kind, loving Him as a small child loves his father, and clinging to Him. As Rav Samson Raphael Hirsch comments on this verse:

> *If everything which we are, which we desire and have — our mind, our body, and our possessions — comes from the love of the one and only G-d, then we, with every fiber of our being, belong to Him, with all that we think, feel, desire, and have. Every thought, every feeling, every power that we have, everything that we possess is a bond that joins us to Him. All that we possess as a pledge of His love, we in turn dedicate to Him as an offering of our love.*

When I contemplated writing a new book, I decided that I would search for people who showed, through their actions, their prayers, and their faith, that they loved Hashem **with all their heart.** In some stories, the subject does not even know that he possesses this level of devotion until he is put to the test and discovers within himself the indomitable love of the Jewish heart for its Father in Heaven. This love is a powerful force within each Jew that has been handed down from our forefathers, from generation to generation. And it has been a great *zechus* for to me to have the opportunity to bring it to light for others to read about, enjoy, and most importantly — to learn from.

But before we begin our journey, I would like to prepare the reader's mind and heart with a panoramic view of the *lev Yehudi* from past to present. Through this collage of short stories and thoughts, a picture emerges of a boundless and eternal love that will, *iy"H*, carry Hashem's chosen people through the rest of history and into the times of Mashiach.

A Fiery Love

Despite the Romans' bitter decree against the learning of Torah, R' Chanina ben Tradyon gathered his *talmidim* every day, in open view, to continue their learning as usual. When the Romans caught R' Chanina, they wrapped him in his Sefer Torah and set him and the scroll on fire. To prolong his agony, the Romans stuffed a clump of wool soaked in water between the scroll and his heart.

Witnessing their rebbi's torturous death, his students asked him, "Rebbi, what do you see?" He replied, "I see the parchment burning, but the letters are flying to heaven."

The commentators explain that R' Chanina was teaching his students that "although the Romans may destroy my body, they can never take my soul." The fiery love of the Jewish *neshamah* for its Creator can never be extinguished. It was a lesson for all time.

In 1942, the Nazis marched into Srulik's town and set out to destroy the Jewish community there, as they had done in every town they entered. They gathered all the Jews in the town square and brought out all the Sifrei Torah of the main shul. The scrolls were still dressed in their elaborate velvet coverings, embroidered with silver and gold.

Abruptly, a Nazi grabbed Srulik, the town barber, and shoved him into the middle of the square where the Sifrei Torah had been stacked.

"Pick it up and take off its covering," the Nazi commanded Srulik, pointing to a scroll dressed in pure white velvet.

Srulik gently lifted the scroll and pressed it close to his chest. The Nazi exploded, "I said undress it! Then throw it on the ground and spit on it and step on it! Do it now or you won't live another minute!"

But Srulik appeared as if he were in a trance. The Nazi's angry rant did not change Srulik's expression at all. Swaying back and forth, he hugged the Torah closer to his heart and kissed it tenderly, like a father kisses a weeping child.

The Nazi opened a container of gasoline that had been brought along to make a bonfire of the Sifrei Torah. He doused Srulik, who still stood there cradling the Torah, and with the flick of a lit matchstick, the Nazi set both Srulik and the Torah ablaze.

Like R' Chanina ben Tradyon, Srulik's love for the Torah would not allow him to betray it, even at the cost of his life. And there is no doubt that if someone were to ask Srulik what he saw at the moment his *neshamah* departed, he would have said, "I see the parchment burning, but the letters are flying to heaven." Our love is eternal, and our *emunah* is steadfast.

A Dance of Emunah

Rabbi Tzvi Hirsch Meisels, the Veitzener Rav, related an episode that occurred while he was in Auschwitz, which demonstrated the powerful *emunah* in the hearts of a group of fifty young men imprisoned there.

It was the night of Simchas Torah, and the Nazis took fifty young men from the camp to the gas chambers. They told the prisoners that they were going to take showers, but they knew the open secret: the showerheads did not emit water, but rather, a deadly gas. As they marched to their destination, they fully realized that very soon, their young lives would be over.

Inside the gas chamber, one of the young men turned to the others and exclaimed, "My dear friends, tonight is Simchas Torah. We do not have a Torah with us tonight, but we do know that the *Ribono Shel Olam* is with us, so let us dance with Him while we still have life."

They formed a circle and instead of carrying Torah scrolls in their arms, they carried Hashem in their hearts. As they danced around the circle, they began to sing, "*Ashreinu ma tov chelkeinu* — How fortunate are we, how good is our lot ..." And they sang, "*Vetaher libeinu* — Purify our heart to serve You ..."

Carried higher and higher by their love of Hashem, their dancing and the singing became so loud that the Nazi guards outside the doors were able to hear it. Rather than the sounds of weeping and wailing they were well accustomed to hearing, they listened in bewilderment to the sounds of joy.

The guards opened the gas-chamber door onto a scenario they could never have expected. On the one hand, they were infuriated by the boys' refusal to succumb to the terror the Nazis were attempting to impose. On the other hand, they could not help but admire the courage of young men dancing and singing in the face of death.

The SS officer in charge asked the boys, "What is the meaning of this nonsense?"

One of the boys replied, "We know that we will be dead in a few minutes. That is why we are so happy. We cannot wait to leave this world that is ruled by dogs like you. Taking leave of loathsome creatures like you is the source of our greatest joy. On top of that, we are overjoyed because we are about to be united with our parents and relatives whom you murdered."

As the boy fearlessly spoke the truth, the officer became increasingly enraged. His pale complexion turned red and his eyes filled with fiery hatred.

"You think you are just going to die and leave this world happy? You won't die so fast, my friends. I will make sure you suffer until you beg to die," he stated. "Out! Out of here all of you. You will stay in a special barracks until I decide what will be done with you."

At this point, the boys had lost all fear. They continued their interrupted dancing within the walls of the gas chamber, until the officer raised his rifle and commanded them to march out. He led them to a barracks where they were placed under guard. There, they were to await their unknown but certainly gruesome fate.

But Hashem had another plan. The next morning, a large group of prisoners was to be transported to another location where their labor was needed. Because there were not enough men to fill the need, most of the fifty boys locked in the barracks were assigned to the transport. They left Auschwitz unharmed. The ones who remained were scattered among the other barracks, where they blended in with the rest of the prisoners. All fifty boys survived the war.

The emunah of these young men defied the laws of nature. Our survival instinct normally makes us fear death, but the faith of these boys empowered their hearts to achieve the unimaginable, finding joy in the opportunity to greet their King.

A Heart Full of Hope

After the war, many survivors found their way to America, where they hoped to rebuild their lives. They knew this would be a very

Rav Beirach Rubinson after the concentration camps and arrival in America (May 1946) (right) — and in his later years (March 22, 1995)

difficult task. Their emotional scars were deep and raw, and their new surroundings posed tremendous challenges. The only answer was *emunah*, as we learn from the story of Reb Beirach Rubinson.

Reb Beirach Rubinson had survived the war with his *emunah* intact. He came to America in 1945 to rebuild his life.

One day shortly after the war, at the offices of Agudath Israel of America in New York, the famed Rabbi Moshe Sherer and Reb Elimelech Tress were sitting together when the door opened upon a shocking sight. There stood a gaunt, skeletal man whose eyes burned with light.

"My name is Beirach Rubinson," the visitor told them. "I would like to find out if there is anything I might be able to do to help the Jews who are still left in Europe."

Despite their boundless efforts on behalf of Europe's Jews, Rabbi Sherer and Reb Elimelech had never before actually seen a survivor. They sat in wonder and awe as Reb Beirach told them the story of all he had been through, of his dreadful imprisonment and the loss of his wife and children.

Suddenly, like a lone star piercing a veil of darkness, his face began to shine with the purest of light. He gazed into the bewildered eyes of his two-man audience and began to sing in a voice that bore the weight of all he had endured: "*Zechor davar l'avdecha al asher yichaltani* — Remember the assurance to Your servant by which You gave me hope. *Zos nechamasi, nechamasi v'anyi, ki imrascha chiyasni* — This is my comfort in my affliction, for Your words have kept me alive" (*Tehillim* 119:49-50).

The words, borne by their haunting tune, penetrated the men's hearts. Then, Reb Beirach's voice gathered strength and soared higher: "*Zeidim helitzuni ad me'od* — These wicked people taunted me and mocked me but ... *mi'Torascha lo natisi* — from Your Torah I have not strayed."

He sang the song again and again, plunging yet deeper each time into the wellspring of faith in his heart. He clasped the hands of Rabbi Sherer and Reb Elimelech and all three began to sing and dance around the small office. With tears streaming down their cheeks, the two Americans beheld this broken man, whose losses were too great to grieve for in an entire lifetime, singing with a heart full of gratitude, "*mi'Torascha lo natisi.*"

It was a vision neither of them would ever forget. Rabbi Sherer turned to Reb Elimelech and said, "With such a *ruach,* these dry bones will come alive again."

Indeed, Reb Beirach came back to life. He re-established himself in America, ultimately settling in Monsey, N.Y., and building a beautiful Torah observant family. By his example of unshakeable *emunah,* he taught many what it means to serve Hashem with joy.

Heart to Heart

Just as we have to love Hashem with all our heart, so too must we love our friends with all our heart. Rav Moshe Sherer was a

Rabbi Sherer addressing the Sixth Knessiah Gedolah. Seated at the dais (l-r): Rabbi Moshe Porush, Rabbi Pinchos Levin, Rabbi Shlomo Zalman Auerbach

person who loved Klal Yisrael with all his heart, and that is why he dedicated his life to serving them.

During his final illness, he received a letter from Rav Avrohom Pam, conveying precisely this message. Rav Pam wrote that he had been thinking about Rav Moshe during the previous Shabbos before Mussaf, when they made the *Mi'shebeirach* prayer, in which one recites: All those who are involved faithfully with the needs of the community, may *Hakadosh Baruch Hu* pay their reward and remove from them every suffering ...

"I thought to myself, *Ribono Shel Olam,* to whom could these words of blessing refer more than Your faithful servant, Moshe ben Basya Bluma? Is there any more faithful activist for our community than he?" Rav Pam's letter related.

We catch a glimpse of Rav Moshe Sherer's legendary *ahavas Yisrael* in the following story:

In the summer of 1995, Rabbi Sherer had just completed his fifth round of chemotherapy. He called his daughter, Mrs. Rochel Langer, and told her that he wanted to make his annual trip to the various Agudah camps in the Catskills. Mrs. Langer knew that her father had been reluctant to see people in his condition, and asked him why he felt compelled to go there.

"I have spoken there for twenty-five years, and I have a message that I feel is very important," he replied.

First, Rabbi Sherer went to speak in the two girls' camps, Camp Bnos and Camp Chayil Miriam. Then he went to speak to the boys in Camp Agudah. Throughout the day, the message remained the same. He told his audiences young and old that their purpose in this world is to improve the life of others, and he urged each one to find ways to take responsibility to help others. At one point he cried out, "As long as I have air in my lungs, I will scream to whoever will listen that we have to live for the next person and not just for ourselves." He then shared examples from the lives of *gedolim,*

The letter from Rabbi Pam

אברהם פאם
RABBI ABRAHAM PAM
582 EAST SEVENTH STREET
BROOKLYN, NEW YORK 11218

בס"ד יום ד' לס' אני ה' רופאך, תשנ"ח

כבוד ידיד נפשי הרב ר' משה שערער שליט"א – שלו' רב לאוי"ט!

ביום שבת שעבר לפני מוסף, כשהתפללנו תפלת "מי שברך" וכל מי שעוסקים בצרכי צבור באמונה הקב"ה ישלם שכרם ויסיר מהם כל מחלה וירפא לכל גופם וכו', אמרתי בלבי: בודאי, למי הדברים מכוונים ומתאימים יותר מעכ"ת הגאון, משה בן חנה בזמנו, כלום יש לך עוסק בצרכי צבור באמונה יותר ממנו?

ובכן, אתפלל ואתי כל ישראל בשוועה אליך, שתסיר ממנו כל מחלה ותשלח לו רפו"ש מן השמים במהרה בתוך שאר חולי ישראל... עד כאן רחשי לבי ותפלתי בלחש ביום ש"ק.

שמעתי פעם מהגאון מוהר"ר חיים קרייזווירטה שליט"א, שיש לשון בירושלמי: "אל תהי ברכת הדיוט קלה בעיניך". ובכן, בני שולח לך ברכתי מעומקא דלבאי [illegible] ברפו"ש ובריאות גופא לאוי"ט, [illegible] כל בית ישראל.

בכבוד ואהבה,

אברהם יעקב הכהן פאם

which illustrate how one can live a life dedicated to the welfare of others.

Before going on his trip to camp, Rabbi Sherer received strict instructions from his doctor to avoid any personal contact, since in his weakened state, he could not afford to contract any kind of infection. Therefore, all staff members and campers were told that they should not attempt to shake Rabbi Sherer's hands when he comes through the dining room to the head table.

As Rabbi Sherer walked through the dining room, passing by each bunk, the staff and campers rose in respect but did not attempt to shake his hand. He maintained his sanitary distance in this way until he came upon bunk *lamed-beis*. There before him were the shining faces of the special-needs children he had worked hard to accommodate at Camp Agudah. He had felt strongly that not only should these children have a camp to enjoy, but the other children should learn from example that special-needs children were an irreplaceable piece of the whole picture of Klal Yisrael.

Rabbi Sherer simply could not resist the *lamed-beis* boys. He went over to one child, shook his hand and wrapped him in a big, friendly hug. Then he did the same for boy after boy, until he had greeted each one.

After he had finished speaking to the camp and had left the dining room, his son, Rabbi Shimshon, who had come to join his father, questioned his decision to make physical contact with the children. "How could you ignore doctor's orders?" he asked. "It could be dangerous for you!"

"Son, these are my children," Rabbi Sherer explained. "You can't deprive a father of hugging his own children. I couldn't help myself."

Reb Shimshon, who had not been allowed to give his father a hug for months, said emotionally, "But Tatte, I am also your son and I want you to give me a hug too."

Rabbi Sherer then gave his son a warm hug. As they embraced, Rabbi Sherer said, "Don't worry my son. There is an *Av*

Harachamim in heaven, and in the merit of founding that special-needs program, I'm going to be cured."

Today, the faith and *ahavas Yisrael* that defined Rabbi Sherer's life still speaks to us, and we still hear his battle call in our ears: "As long as I have air in my lungs, I will scream to whoever will listen that we have to live for the next person and not just for ourselves."

For the Love of Torah

We express our love for Hashem by learning His Torah and following its mitzvos. Learning Torah is our primary occupation in life, and Hashem made it a pleasant occupation, teaching that the words of Torah are *masok mi'devash* — sweeter then honey.

Rav Aharon Leib Shteinman

Yet there is a great deal of effort required to uncover that sweetness, and for some people. the taste never seems to emerge. They find it impossible to devote themselves, with all their heart, to what feels like a futile effort. In this story, Rav Aharon Leib Shteinman helps one *bachur* get to the root of the problem.

A *bachur* asked his rebbi, "Could Rebbi please bring me to the home of

Rav Aharon Leib Shteinman so that I can ask him a question that's been bothering me?"

The rebbi agreed to accompany his student.

"There's just one other thing," the student said. "Could Rebbi please agree to let me speak to Rav Shteinman without interruption?" The rebbi agreed to the condition.

A few days later, the rebbi and his *talmid* were seated in Rav Shteinman's office. The Rav invited the boy to ask his question.

"Does the Rosh Yeshivah like steak?" the boy asked.

Rav Shteinman replied, "What is steak?"

The *bachur* replied that it was a very choice piece of meat. Rav Shteinman said he wasn't familiar with it.

"Perhaps I will bring the Rosh Yeshivah a piece of steak so that he can experience its delicous taste," the *bachur* suggested.

There was a long silence. The rebbi felt a mounting discomfort as the *bachur* seemed to have nothing more in mind than wasting the Rosh Yeshivah's precious time. The boy then asked another question.

"Does the Rosh Yeshivah like ice cream?"

Again, Rav Shteinman admitted his ignorance of another culinary pleasure, and again, the boy offered to enlighten him with his first taste of it. "If the Rosh Yeshivah tastes it, he will see how good it is," the *bachur* stated.

At this point, Rav Shteinman looked at the *bachur's* rebbi and asked, "What does he want from me?"

But the boy quickly turned to his rebbi and reminded him, "You promised you wouldn't interrupt our conversation!"

Then the boy turned to Rav Shteinman and, with a voice edging on tears, told him, "I have been in yeshivah for nearly ten years, and I simply can't find my place. Everyone keeps telling me that I have to experience the sweetness of Torah, but I don't feel anything.

"The Rosh Yeshivah doesn't have a taste for steak or ice cream, and has no desire to taste them even though I am telling him how good they are. So too, I have no taste for my learning, even though everyone is telling me how good it can be. I don't know what people want from my life!"

The *bachur* stared at Rav Shteinman, hoping to hear something that would give him some inner peace.

The Rosh Yeshivah asked him, "What is the sweetest food in the world?

The *bachur* thought for a moment and replied, "Honey."

Rav Shteinman asked, "Is it possible for anyone to say that honey is bitter? Only someone who is foolish would say such a thing."

The *bachur* nodded his head in agreement.

Rav Shteinman continued, "But even a smart person would agree that sometimes honey can taste bitter. When a person has sores in his mouth, then even honey, which is intrinsically sweet, will burn his mouth and taste bitter to him.

"Young man, I do not know you, but it is possible that on your lips are spiritual wounds that are causing the sweetness of the Torah to taste bitter for you. *Lashon hara, nivul peh,* and *sheker* are the types of wounds that tend to cause a lot of bitterness and destroy the sweetness of learning. Heal those wounds and you will begin to taste the sweetness of Torah."

Rav Shteinman was teaching this bachur that if we want to truly develop a love for Torah, we have to try our best to heal the spiritual wounds that might be preventing our growth. The sweetness is there for us to attain, but we have to work on clearing away the spiritual obstacles in order to experience it.

Learning at All Costs

Rav Shmuel Berenbaum, Rosh Yeshivah of Brooklyn's Mirrer Yeshivah, was known for his incredible *ahavas haTorah* and *has-*

Rav Shmuel Berenbaum learning Torah on the helicopter

madah baTorah. The learning *seder* in the yeshivah was inviolable, and *talmidim* knew that if they wanted Rav Shmuel to officiate at a wedding, the *chuppah* would have to take place after 8 p.m. so that it would not interfere with the yeshivah's learning schedule.

Once, Rav Shmuel was informed that the wedding of one of his granddaughters would be taking place in Lakewood, N.J. Rav Shmuel knew that the time required to travel to Lakewood would force him to leave yeshivah before the end of second *seder*. He asked his family why the wedding had to take place in Lakewood rather than in Brooklyn. He was told that a Brooklyn wedding would cost an additional $5,000.

"I am willing to give $5,000 toward the wedding expenses so that it can take place in Brooklyn and I will not have to miss second *seder* in yeshivah," offered Rav Shmuel. The wedding was held in Brooklyn and Rav Shmuel did not miss his precious second *seder*.

On another occasion, Rav Shmuel was invited to give a *shiur* in a *kollel* in Philadelphia. In order to minimize the Rosh Yeshivah's time away from the yeshivah, a helicopter was hired to take Rav

Shmuel to his destination. One of the most inspiring pictures I have ever seen was taken on that trip. In it, Rav Shmuel sits in the helicopter doing what he always did: learning Torah.

I think it's safe to say that 99.9 percent of humanity would experience their first helicopter ride in a different way. They would either be holding on in fear or enjoying the beautiful view from above. But for Rav Shmuel, it didn't matter whether he was in the *beis midrash* in his seat, traveling by car, or flying hundreds of feet in the air. Only one thing mattered: Torah, Torah, and more Torah. I believe he was teaching us all a most powerful lesson.

"Tov li Toras picha mei'alfei zahav va'chesef — Your Torah is more precious to me than all the gold and silver in the world."

Million Dollar Moments

I conclude with one final vignette. During Chol HaMoed Pesach, my father-in-law told me that if I wanted to experience a really inspiring davening, I should come to the *minyan* of Rav Don Segal in Boro Park,

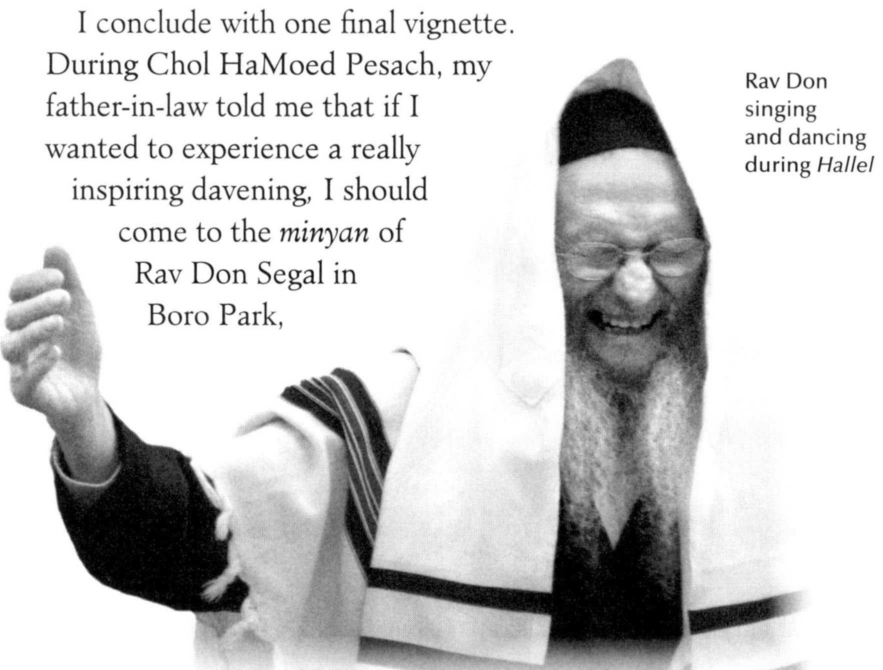

Rav Don singing and dancing during *Hallel*

Brooklyn. Rav Don was visiting from Eretz Yisrael and was conducting a *minyan* in a shul on 18th Avenue.

I was told that the *minyan* reaches its peak during *Hallel*, when Rav Don, who leads the davening, erupts with joy as he reaches the words, "*Hodu Lashem ki tov* — Give thanks to Hashem for He is good." His overflowing *simchah* inspires him to dance, and the shul fills with energy as the congregants are caught up by his enthusiasm.

I came to the shul and found a room filled with people who, like myself, hoped to experience a really special davening. The *tefillos* went along in a fairly ordinary manner until we reached *Hallel*. When Rav Don broke into singing and dancing, I was mesmerized. He had so much *simchah* and love when he said *Hodu Lashem* that the joy in the air was palpable. The only description I can offer is that he looked as ecstatic as someone who has just won a million dollars.

I decided that this was a scene I needed to capture on camera, so that I could always look at it for inspiration. It would be a permanent reminder of the level of joy a person can reach in his service of Hashem. And so, on the next day of Chol HaMoed, I brought my camera to shul, and the moment he began to sing *Hodu*, I took that million-dollar picture.

The *Maharal* says that Hashem is constantly taking pictures of our million-dollar moments. They are the moments when He sees that we have reached our potential in a certain area or have overcome a certain test. He, too, holds onto these pictures and looks at them from time to time to remind Himself of how special and precious we really are.

We live in a time when we are constantly bombarded by advertisements and attractions that promise us the world and vie for our heart. But we know that Hashem wants our heart. Thus we are tested daily: to whom shall we give our heart? In what will we invest our energies and abilities — our bodies or our souls?

When you read in this collection of stories about people like you and me who give Hashem everything they have, I hope that you, too, will be inspired to give Hashem not only your heart, but to serve him **with all your heart**

In turn, may Hashem grant us all of our hearts' desires, and bless us with a life of *berachah*, *hatzlachah*, and *kol tuv*.

Acknowledgments

It is with a deep sense of gratitude that I present my sixth book of inspirational stories to the public. Whenever I embark on a new book, I pray to Hashem that He will guide me to the stories that will deliver the right message to the readers. I also try to find a different focus for each book, as everyone likes a *chiddush*, myself included. It was with that thought in mind that I began to search for stories of people who served Hashem with all their heart. *Baruch Hashem,* there was a lot of *siyata d'Shmaya* along the way, and I am thrilled that I was successful in finding a collection of heartwarming stories of devotion and inspiration.

These are stories of people who served Hashem in a unique way, or believed in Him even when it was very difficult to do so. They prayed to Him from the depths of their heart when there seemingly was no way out of their troubles, and they were answered. These are stories of *gedolim* and stories about your next-door neighbor. These are stories of people who truly lived up to the dictate, "You shall love Hashem ***with all your heart.***"

Writing a book of this nature is not something one can do alone. It takes a lot of teamwork. Therefore, I would to take this opportunity to thank the many people who gave me stories or advised me regarding certain aspects of this book, helping to make it a reality.

Rabbi Duvi Bensoussan (Lakewood), Rabbi Tuvia Steinharter (Lakewood), Rabbi Moshe Rubin (Staten Island), Rabbi Dani Staum (Monsey), Rabbi Zecharia Wallerstein (Brooklyn), Reb Shmuli Kott (Lakewood), Reb Michoel and Reb Avi Pruzansky (Brooklyn, Passaic), Rabbi Fishel Schachter (Brooklyn), Rabbi Ari Pruzansky

(Lakewood), Rabbi Dovid Juravel (Monsey), Rabbi Shmuel Zev Juravel (South Fallsburg), Rabbi Mordechai Grunwald (Brooklyn), Rabbi Ari Fireman (Monsey), Reb Buddy Berkowitz (Lakewood), Reb Yehuda Dershowitz (Lakewood), Rabbi Zalman Feuer (Lakewood), Mrs. Chavie Bauman (Lakewood), Reb Shmully Sussman (Chicago).

Special thanks goes to **Rabbi Benzion Klatzko,** who has been a great friend and a source of stories from the beginning of this series. Our friendship led me to spend a Shabbos at the Klatzko home in Monsey, together with a group of secular college students. It was a very heartwarming Shabbos and afterward I realized that the *frum* world would benefit just as much by experiencing an uplifting Shabbos that was geared especially to them. This led me to launch **Revach,** an organization that arranges inspirational *Shabbatonim* and events for the *frum* community.

In order for a story to have the right impact on a reader, you need the right word, phrase, or approach in presenting the story. I am lucky to have **Mrs. Chana Nestlebaum** as the editor of this book. She is a master of the written word, and has taken my stories and polished them with expertise and precision. The success of this entire series has a lot to do with her incredible work and devotion. May Hashem bless her with continued *berachah, hatzlachah,* and *kol tuv.*

I am once again honored to have my book published in the Artscroll Series. **Rabbi Meir Zlotowitz** and **Rabbi Nosson Scherman** have given their heart and soul to spreading inspiration throughout the world through the publication of a broad variety of Torah literature that has made an impact on countless Jews. May they continue their great work of *harbatzas haTorah* with good health and success.

The **Artscroll team** has done a terrific job in creating a beautiful book from start to finish. Their professionalism can be seen throughout and it greatly enhances this work. Thank you, **Rabbi Avrohom Biderman,** for always being there for me and for your good advice. Thank you, **Reb Mendy Herzberg,** for coordinating the entire project and seeing it through. Thank you, **Mrs. Mindy Stern,** for your insightful editing and comments. Thank you, **Reb Eli Kroen,** for producing a very creative and striking cover design. Thank you, **Miss Devorah Bloch** and **Miss Rivky Plittman** for doing a fantastic job in paginating the book.

To my Rav, **Rabbi Gavriel Finkel**, who has been a true source of *chizuk* and inspiration for me, thank you.

My parents, **Reb Yosef** and **Marsha Pruzansky,** are great role models and have always been there for me and my *mishpachah*. May they have continued *nachas* from all their children and grandchildren.

My in-laws, **Rabbi Shmuel Gedaliah** and **Raizel Pollak,** are everything a son-in-law can ask for. May they have continued *nachas* from the entire *mishpachah*.

Finally, I would like to thank my wife **Rochie** for her constant support in all my endeavors. Writing books takes a lot of time and effort, and it is only with her patience and encouragement that I have been able to take on various projects of *harbatzas Torah*. May Hashem bless us with much *nachas* and *berachah* from our dear children.

It is my sincere hope that this book will inspire and uplift those who read it, and may we all merit to serve Hashem **with all our heart**.

Binyomin Pruzansky
Lakewood N.J.
Av 5772 / August 2012

DOCUMENT AND PHOTO CREDITS

Agudath Israel of America
R' Yehuda Eckstein
Tsemach Glenn
Shmuli Sussman

Chapter 1:

Believing in Hashem With All Your Heart

A Yearning Heart

The following incredible story was related by Rabbi Duvi Bensoussan in a lecture during the Nine Days, which mark the period of mourning leading up to Tishah B'Av, the day on which the First and Second Temples were destroyed. It teaches us what it really means to wait for and yearn for the coming of Mashiach. The Chofetz Chaim writes that this longing, in and of itself, is a merit that helps to bring the Final Redemption one step closer.

When I was 19 years old, my days were spent learning Torah in Yeshivas Itri, an Israeli yeshivah located in the Talpiot section of Yerushalayim. I often traveled to and from yeshivah on Bus 21, a local city bus that traveled up and down a busy thoroughfare called Derech Chevron. The route led through the center of town and terminated at the Kotel.

There was a rumor — more like a legend — about Derech Chevron. My friends told me that it was well known that a young Sefardi boy, perhaps about 8 years old, held a vigil on the street. He was a pure, innocent soul, a child of *baalei teshuvah,* who had not absorbed even one drop of doubt or cynicism about the coming of Mashiach. Therefore, each day at the conclusion of his yeshivah classes, he would descend a massive staircase that led to Derech Chevron, come out to the curb and peer down the road to his left, checking to see if Mashiach was on his way.

He looked only to the left because in that direction, Derech Chevron led to the resting place of Rachel Imeinu. His rebbi had told the class that when Mashiach comes to Yerushalayim, he will ride his white donkey past Kever Rochel to tell her that her prayers for her children have been answered. Therefore, the boy reasoned that if he stood on Derech Chevron, looking in the direction of Kever Rochel, he could not miss the coming of Mashiach.

I thought it was a nice story, a touching story. Nevertheless, I told my friends that I had to see it myself. Hoping to see living proof of this legendary child, I would always glance out the window of the bus as we passed the staircase on Derech Chevron, but I never caught sight of the boy. Despite my friends' insistence that the story was true, I was beginning to believe that it was nothing more than a fanciful tale.

Despite my doubt, my eyes were irresistibly drawn to the window whenever I rode Bus 21 past the staircase. One day, on my way back to yeshivah from the Kotel, I glanced out the window and caught sight of a young boy running down the stairs. Was that him? I couldn't believe my eyes. I quickly pressed the button, alerting the driver that I wanted to get off the bus. He stopped a block away and I leaped out the door and charged up the street toward the stairs.

I watched as the boy purposefully ran down the steps, as if he were rushing to catch a bus. I tried to look casual, as if I myself were waiting for a bus. My plan was just to watch him and see what he did. After a few moments, though, I could not contain my curiosity. I approached him and summoned up my best Israeli accent to ask him, "Little boy, what are you waiting for?"

The boy looked me up and down and asked, "Are you American?"

"Yes."

"Don't worry. It's nothing," he said dismissively.

"Really, *b'emet,* little boy, please tell me what are you looking for," I pleaded.

"Nah, it's nothing at all ..."

"Please, please I really have to know," I asked yet again. I stood there expectantly.

Finally, the boy's expression softened. He somehow knew that I would not ridicule his answer.

"Every day I come down these steps, and I wait here to see if Mashiach is coming that day," he stated simply, all the while watching my face for a response.

"I know that one day soon Mashiach will come," I told the boy. "And when he does, you will be in the front of the line of those who come to greet him. But let me ask you something. On that great day when Mashiach finally arrives and you meet him, what will you say to him?"

"What will I say to him?" the boy repeated, as if the question had the most obvious answer in the world. "I will ask him 'Why did you take so long to come? I have been waiting for you so anxiously!' "

That is the pure emunah that our nation still carries in its heart after 2,000 years of exile. How can Hashem not count as a tremendous merit our undying devotion as we stand our ground through centuries of war and persecution, steadfastly "waiting at the curb" until he comes to take us home? In this merit, may we be privileged to stand alongside this young boy to greet Mashiach Tzidkeinu, bimheirah veyameinu.

Opening the Gates

When the heavenly gates are open, one must take the opportunity to walk through. To take advantage of these moments, we have to be cognizant of their arrival. Sometimes it's a special occasion, sometimes it's a good deed, and sometimes it's an elevated neshamah that creates these propitious times for spiritual connection. In this story, Rabbi Benzion Klatzko introduces us to a young man whose great merit opened the gates for all who wanted to pass through.

One Shabbos, we were hosting around eighty college students at our home, hoping to give them a chance to absorb the beauty of this central part of Jewish life. During the Shabbos *seudah*, I explained the concept of an *eis ratzon* — a propitious time when the gates of heaven are open wide to our prayers. As a stark example of this concept, I told them about a tremendously moving moment that I spent with my 19-year-old nephew, Raphael Moshe Mattisyahu Juravel that week.

During this time, my nephew was bedridden with his second relapse of a vicious cancer. He had been taken to Boston to a top specialist for his first round of chemotherapy, and our hopes were raised high when the illness seemed to go into remission. In fact, we made a grand *seudas hodaah* (a meal of thanksgiving) for him, and he rose to his feet to thank Hashem from the bottom of his heart.

Unfortunately, it was not long before the disease came back with a vengeance. He underwent another round of treatment, and miraculously, it seemed to rid him of the disease. Once again, however, the cancer reappeared, this time more forcefully than ever.

A short while after this relapse, my son and I were summoned to come to his room to help make a *minyan*. We arrived and joined the group of men, each of whom was given a paper bearing a prayer I had never seen before. The words shook me to the core:

"We ten people who are bringing the *Shechinah* (Divine Presence) to this room where the sick person is, we declare if there ever was a curse put upon this boy, we remove it. If there ever was a *cheirem* (excommunication) we remove it. If there ever was a dream about this boy that was translated in a negative way, we remove it. If there ever was an *ayin hara* (evil eye) on this boy we remove it ..."

When we were done reciting the prayer, someone handed Moshe Mattisyahu a *siddur* and asked him to recite "*Nishmas kol chai,*" which we say on Shabbos. Our hearts ached as we watched this young man open his heart to Hashem and plead for his life. He knew that the doctors had given up hope and had advised his parents to simply keep him as comfortable as possible until the end. Yet he did not despair; doctors were only human. He turned his heart toward Heaven and delivered his entire being into Hashem's hands, begging with each word of prayer to see Hashem's salvation.

As witnesses to this soul-searing scene, we knew that at that moment, in that room, the gates of Heaven were flung open wide. We knew that our own prayers, joined to those of my nephew, would ascend unimpeded and arrive at the very foot of the Heavenly Throne. This was an *eis ratzon* of intense power.

The story of my nephew's prayers made a deep impact on the college students. They were clearly touched by his unwavering faith and bravery. When our Shabbos meal was concluded, a student named Shyka came to me and asked if he and his friend could visit Moshe Mattisyahu that afternoon. Since my nephew's house was only a 10-minute walk from my home, I encouraged him to go ahead.

Soon after *bentching*, Shyka and his friend headed toward the door. By now, though, the rest of the group had heard about their visit and wanted to join. Soon, there were 25 students amassed outside my front door, getting ready to set out to my nephew's home. I quickly reassessed my plans to take a much-needed Shabbos nap, and decided that this was a moment not to be missed. With 25 people embarking together on the mitzvah of *bikur cholim*, the gates of Heaven were bound to fly open once again, and I had to be there.

As we began to walk down the block, more and more students joined us. By the time we reached the end of the block, there were 60 students altogether — an amazing parade of soldiers seeking to do the Will of Hashem.

When we arrived at the house, I told my in-laws that I brought a few guests to visit Moshe Mattisyahu. They welcomed us but urged me to check with my nephew to see if he wanted visitors.

When I went to his room, I saw that he was clearly feeling weak. Nevertheless, when I explained to him that this was a large group that would be greatly strengthened in their connection with *Yiddishkeit* through this experience, he consented. "But what should I tell them?" he asked.

"You don't have to tell them anything," I assured him.

I went to the kitchen and found some carrots and celery sticks which I could use to make a *berachos* party with my students. Having someone answer amen to a *berachah* is a known *segulah* for salvation, and salvation was what my nephew needed.

"Okay," I announced. "We will go around the room, each person here will make a *berachah* on his food, and we will all answer 'Amen.'" Many students had to be taught the *berachah* and it took a while to go around the room. When we finished, I thanked Moshe Mattisyahu for allowing us to visit, and knowing how weak he was, advised him that we would be leaving so that he could get some much needed rest. Moshe Mattisyahu interjected, "How come you're leaving after only making *ha'adamah* (the *berachah* for vegetables). Let's get some more food so we can make more *berachos*."

We quickly brought to the room a pitcher of water and some pretzels, and the *berachos* party began anew. One by one, each person said his *berachah* and the rest of us in the room answered "Amen." I could see the color returning to Moshe Mattisyahu's face as each amen echoed off the walls.

Suddenly, from the back of the room, someone began to sing a moving song: "*Orech yamim asbi'eihu v'areihu bishuasi* — I will satiate him with long days, and will show him salvation ...."

As this young man's song began to spread around the room, the students who knew it chanted the words. Those who didn't know the song hummed the tune. The song, together with all the *berachos* that had been said, created an atmosphere of holiness that was palpable to all.

Suddenly I called out, "Is there a Kohen in the room?" A boy raised his hand.

"Come to the front and give my nephew a *berachah*," I suggested.

"But what should I say?" the boy asked. He had never said the *Bircas Kohanim* before.

So word for word, I said and he repeated the *berachah* of peace given to Aharon HaKohen.

By this time, Moshe Mattisyahu had forgotten his pain and was sitting up in bed smiling, excited by all the *zechusim* being amassed. However, he still needed his rest and soon it was time for us to go.

"Thanks, Moshe Mattisyahu. We really appreciate the chance to come and spend time with you. Have a good Shabbos," I told him. As the crowd began moving out of the room, he called us back.

"Wait! You forgot to make a *berachah acharonah*!" he implored.

So back we went, cramming into the room once more to provide one more amen in the merit of our host. Then I leaned over his bed, hugged his frail body, and planted a kiss on his forehead. "You have opened the gates for each of us! Do you see how important you are? Do you see how much we need you? Thanks for letting us come," I told him.

Just then, the boy who had started the singing pushed his way through the group over to where I was standing by my nephew's bedside. I realized at that moment that the song had been coming from Shyka, the one who had initiated this entire venture.

"Rabbi, I want to tell you something important," he said with urgency. "I want you to know that I was born in Bnei Brak and went to a regular yeshivah and was once *shomer Shabbos*. But when I left for America, I left my *Yiddishkeit* behind. I have not kept Shabbos in eight years. But Rabbi, I must tell you that I feel that the gates are open and I must walk through! I will keep Shabbos from now on."

Then another voice was heard. "I will also start keeping Shabbos, because I also want to walk through the gates." Another young man said, "I have a one-man band, and the next time I play at a wedding, I am going to give all the money I earn to *tzedakah*."

The gates were opened, and one by one, each student announced his or her burning desire to walk through. We all thanked Moshe Mattisyahu and left his presence feeling uplifted and inspired. We all knew that we had changed for the better. We had walked through the gates and felt closer to Hashem than ever.

Unfortunately, a few weeks after this memorable Shabbos, Moshe Mattisyahu returned his pure and precious soul to his Creator. But he left behind an everlasting legacy. He toiled in Torah day and night until the very end. His love for Torah and mitzvos was extraordinary. The following story defines who Moshe Mattisyahu was:

In the last months of his life, Moshe Mattisyahu had the opportunity to go to Eretz Yisrael with a very special Jew named Reb Eli Rowe. It was not simple to get Moshe Mattisyahu to Eretz Yisrael, as there was a lot of equipment that had to be brought along, but Eli arranged everything.

Once Moshe Mattisyahu got there, he was eager to search the *sefarim* stores for volumes that can only be found in Eretz Yisrael. And of course, he went to visit the illustrious *gedolim* of the land, seeking *berachos* to help his situation. On a visit to Rav Chaim Kanievsky, Moshe Mattisyahu was able to ask a question that had been bothering him for a long time.

He explained to Rav Chaim that his sickness had destroyed his body to the point where he no longer had any feeling from his waist down. His problem was that, although he loved to learn Torah more than anything in the world, he knew that the halachah prohibits people from learning in an unclean state. The paralysis of his lower body left him unaware of the sensation of expelling waste, and thus, he could easily trespass the halachah unintentionally. He wanted to know if, in this case, he was still allowed to learn Torah.

Rav Chaim thought for a moment, and then answered that he may continue to learn even though he could not know if he was fit to do so according to halachah. Moshe Mattisyahu greeted Rav Chaim's answer with pure joy, because now he could learn without any hesitation.

Rav Chaim Kanievsky

After Moshe Mattisyahu left, a witness to the scene asked Rav Chaim how he had come to his decision. Rav Chaim explained, "The reason you can't learn Torah when you are not clean is because it is a disgrace to the Torah. However, whenever this boy learns Torah, it is not possible for it to be a disgrace. Rather, it is the world's greatest honor for the Torah when such a boy learns."

Yehi zichro baruch. May we all learn from Moshe Mattisyahu to take advantage of every moment in this world, and to take every opportunity to walk through the gates when they are open.

Bringing Heaven to Earth

When one calls out to Hashem in a time of great need, he is expressing his belief that Hashem alone is the source of his salvation. His prayer for rescue from what seems to be an intrac-

table, impossible situation is actually a request for Hashem to change the natural course on earth. The holy sefarim explain that a person's level of salvation is equal to his level of emunah. It is up to us to realize that we have the ability, through our prayers, to bring Heaven's unlimited stores of goodness down to earth.

Little Yitzchok Minchik* was a bright, lively child. At the age of 5, however, he began to lose weight and energy. The sparkle faded from his eyes and the color from his complexion. Alarmed at their son's decline, his parents brought him to doctors throughout Israel, seeking a treatment. Sadly, no one seemed to be able to offer any hope. The parents watched in helpless despair as their beautiful little boy faded away.

During the entire ordeal Rabbi Minchik, Yitzchok's father, had gotten in touch with every medical referral agency in Israel, hoping that one of them would be able to direct him to a doctor who could help his son. The agencies all tried valiantly, contacting doctors not only in Israel but in America and elsewhere, hoping to find the right address for the rapidly declining little boy.

One day, the call Rabbi Minchik had longed for finally came.

"This is Motti Schwartz* from Bikur Cholim," said an enthusiastic voice on the phone. "We have found an American doctor who we feel can help your son, but you will have to act very quickly if you want to meet him."

A rush of adrenalin instantly energized Rabbi Minchik. "Tell me what I have to do," he said. "I'm ready right now!"

"You need to get to Bnei Brak to see a man named Doctor Steiner. He's here visiting from the U.S., but he's leaving for the airport in a half-hour. He said he would wait for you until then, so you had better get going immediately."

"A half-hour? But it takes at least 45 minutes to get to Bnei Brak!" Rabbi Minchik exclaimed.

"Just move as fast as you can." Motti Schwartz urged him. "Maybe you'll be lucky."

His hands shaking with nervousness, Rabbi Minchik wrote down the address, gathered up his limp, gaunt child in his arms, and ran out to the street to catch a cab. He felt a small charge of optimism when a cab stopped for him almost immediately. Maybe things would go his way, he thought.

"I need to be in Bnei Brak by 5," he told the driver urgently. "I know it's late. But here's 400 *shekel* for you — just go as fast as you can! It's really a matter of life and death."

The driver took on the challenge and wove through traffic expertly, finally reaching the highway, which he navigated at top speed. Rabbi Minchik knew the driver was doing his best, yet he could not help urging him on. "Please, please!" he pleaded. "I have just this one chance to see this doctor, and he's the only one who can save my son!"

It was 5:15 when the cab pulled up in front of the designated address. Rabbi Minchik's heart was pounding, his muscles taut with tension as he paid the driver and swept his son into his arms. Despite the oppressive heat of summer, he ran at full speed up two flights of stairs to the third-floor apartment where the doctor was staying, and banged on the door shouting, "Hello! I'm here!"

When the apartment owner opened the door, he beheld a breathless, sweat-soaked man with a desperate look in his eyes and a small, pale child lying motionless in his arms.

"Hi, I'm here to see Doctor Steiner," Rabbi Minchik panted. "Is he still here?"

"Oh, I am very sorry, but he left 5 minutes ago to the airport," the man informed him. "He said he was waiting for someone to meet him, but he could not wait any longer as he was afraid he would miss his flight."

The color drained from Rabbi Minchik's face as he absorbed the man's words. Up until that moment, he had not entertained any possibility other than that somehow, his extreme effort would prove worthwhile. Somehow, Hashem would stop the clock or hold the doctor back. But no — nature had taken its normal course. A 45-minute ride had taken 45 minutes, and a man who had a plane to catch had left for the airport.

A wave of vertigo overtook Rabbi Minchik as the superhuman energy he had called upon for this effort ebbed away like a receding tide, and the heat, exertion, and tension finally caught up with him. He looked as though he might faint.

"Please, come in and rest," the man told him. "Have a cold glass of water."

The downcast Rabbi Minchik marched unsteadily into the apartment, gently lowered his son onto the couch and sat down next to him. "How could it be?" he thought. "Five minutes late! If I had only gotten the call a few minutes sooner. If the cab driver had only run into fewer red lights. If he had only been able to go a little faster — we would have made it and my son would be on his way to a *refuah*.

"And now what's left? I will have to go to America, but how? I don't have money for such a trip, and imagine what the treatment will cost!"

As his mind wandered morosely over the events of the past hour, his host walked in and handed him a cold glass of water. He held it up in his right hand and pronounced out loud, *"Baruch Atah Hashem, Elokeinu Melech haolam, shehakol nih'yeh bidvaro."*

As he took the first revitalizing sip of water, the words he had just spoken began to reverberate in his mind. With a sudden shock of realization, he froze in his place, holding his glass in mid-route to his mouth. Of course! *Hakol* — everything — comes into being through the word of Hashem! Here I am chasing down this doctor, telling the cab driver that the doctor is the only one who can save my son. Why am I not chasing down the only One Who really *can* save my son? Why am I not running and sweating and racing against the clock to pray?

As this realization took hold, Rabbi Minchik began to relax. He had not missed his chance; his chance to help his son was still there and was always there. A sense of peace and confidence washed over the aching heart of this loving father. Hashem was in control, and everything would be fine.

When Rabbi Minchik returned with his son to Yerushalayim, his efforts took a new direction. While he still sought a doctor to help deliver the cure, he directed his most ardent efforts to addressing the Creator of all cures. Within a few months of his nerve-shattering trip to Bnei Brak, a medical referral agency put him in touch with a doctor right there in Israel who could treat his son's condition. Indeed, after a few months of rigorous treatment, little Yitzchok Minchik was cured. His parents marveled at the rebirth of their precious son.

Shortly after Yitzchok was declared healthy, Rabbi Minchik made a *seudas hodaah* to celebrate the miracle. The speech Rabbi Minchik made centered on his journey to Bnei Brak — a seemingly fruitless effort that in fact, directed him to the only strategy that could help. He recalled how the *berachah* on the glass of water awakened him to Hashem's primary role as the Force behind everything from the disease to the cure. It was that realization, he was certain, that brought him to pray with the total sincerity and devotion needed to bring Hashem's cure down from heaven.

Everyone at the *seudah* was touched by the speech, but one guest asked Rabbi Minchik, "If the answer to your problems was realizing *shekol nih'yeh bidvaro,* then why did you have to go through the trouble of traveling to Bnei Brak? You could have drunk a glass of water at home in Yerushalayim and realized the same thing!"

"In Yerushalyim, I would never have discovered that simple truth," Rabbi Minchik answered. "What I went through made me realize how completely I was counting on the doctor. I kept saying, and I felt, that he was the only one who could cure my son. I had to make the desperate trip and suffer the disappointment in order to be open to the lesson Hashem wanted to teach me.

In Bnei Brak, the words were a contrast to everything I had just done. In Yerushalayim, it would have just been a glass of water."

> *Sometimes we take a trip, thinking that it is the road to our destination. But we may find out that in reality, it is a detour that puts our lives back on to the road to success. We must always realize that a strong sense of emunah is the ultimate GPS for life. It will forever steer us in the right direction without us ever having to recalculate.*

> *This story reminds me of a riveting account of emunah that helped save a group of non-religious soldiers at war, when they realized "shehakol nih'yeh bidvaro."*

The Yom Kippur War was raging. A group of Israeli soldiers huddled in their tank, fighting for their lives against an Egyptian force that outnumbered them ten to one. The enemy, determined to crush the tiny Jewish nation into oblivion, pressed on with full force. The tank captain began to realize that the situation was hopeless. Sweat shone on his face and fear paralyzed the crew as they came to terms with the fact that, short of a miracle, nothing could save them. Heavy artillery and antitank missiles bit into the ground all around them, and mere moments stood between life and the inevitable, fatal strike to their tank.

Desperately, the crew commander screamed, "Is there anyone here who knows how to pray to G-d to save us? Can anyone help us pray?"

"Rafi might be able to help us," shouted one of the crew members in reply. "He's *dati* (religious)!"

"Rafi, come over here and help us pray!" ordered the commander.

A pale young man crawled to the front of the tank, trying to mask his deep fear. "My grandfather used to stress the power of a *berachah* pronounced with proper concentration," he managed. "He'd give us a cup of milk, and ask us to say the *berachah* aloud, so that everyone in the room could answer 'Amen.' Then he would tell us that we were protected for that entire day."

He swallowed hard, reached into his uniform pocket and produced a candy. "I'm going to make a *berachah* on this candy, and each of you must answer 'Amen' with all his heart. Perhaps the merit of the *berachah* will save us."

The tank crew's eyes fixed on Rafi as he held the candy up, and shouted, "*Baruch Atah Hashem, Elokeinu Melech haolam, shehakol nih'yeh bidvaro!*"

"AMEN!" thundered every member of the tank crew, as the piercing whistle of heavy artillery sounded all around them.

"Now back to your positions!" ordered the commander.

The tank crew attacked with renewed faith and vigor. Somehow, every shot they fired seemed to destroy a significant target, while every missile lobbed their way turned out to be a dud, or missed them entirely. Incredibly, the battle began to turn, and the Egyptian forces fell back.

The Israelis scored a crushing victory that day, and it was widely acknowledged as a miraculous, unnatural one. The one *berachah* on the battlefield seemed to have formed an invisible shield over the soldiers, protecting them against impossible odds.

These stories illustrate the power of a berachah to protect us and bring salvation in difficult times. However there is another important aspect to a berachah — it is a means by which we can connect to our Father in Heaven. Reciting a berachah expresses our innate desire to have a close relationship with Hashem, as we learn from the following story related by Rav Yitzchok Zilberstein.

As I got off the bus from Yerushalayim at the Tel Aviv bus station and headed toward the exit, my eyes caught sight of an unusual scene. About twenty non-religious schoolchildren were standing around their teacher. An elderly *chareidi* man approached them and pulled a candy out of his pocket. He walked over to one of the children and asked, "Would you like a candy?"

The child nodded eagerly.

"Okay, you can have it," he said. "Only first, you must make a *berachah — "Shehakol nih'yeh bidvaro."*

The boy agreed. The elderly man guided him through the words of the *berachah,* and then pronounced an enthusiastic "Amen" at its conclusion.

When the boy's friends saw that the old man was giving out candy, they flocked around him like clamoring geese. Oddly, however, they were not clamoring for the candy.

"I want to make a *berachah!"* they were shouting. "Me, too! I want to make a *berachah* too!" Twenty little boys stood there, holding out their hands for candy so that they could also make a *berachah.*

The elderly man had come prepared. He reached into his pocket and extracted a big fistful of candies. He asked the boys to stand in line, take a candy, and hold onto it for a few moments so that they could all make a *berachah* together. The children followed his instructions, and when everyone had a candy in his hand, the man had them repeat the *berachah* word by word after him.

As if they were cheering for their favorite team, they shouted each word together. The man answered "Amen" with equal enthusiasm, and the children, giggling with delight, opened their candies and popped them into their mouths.

Meanwhile, the children's teacher was watching the scene with a combination of amusement and confusion. Why were the children so excited about making a *berachah*? Most of them barely knew what a *berachah* was!

I walked over to where the teacher was standing and introduced myself with a hearty *shalom aleichem.*

"Could I share a story with you that the great *Mashgiach,* Rav Elyah Lopian, used to tell? I think it would explain what was going on here with the children."

"Sure," the teacher answered, still gazing with bewilderment at his class. And so, I began:

The story took place during the Inquisition. At that time, a Jewish child was snatched from his home and was taken into the custody of the church, where he was forced to convert. As the years went by and he showed his intelligence, the church officials entered him into training to become a priest. He excelled at his job and rose in the ranks until he was appointed Chief Judge of the church.

In that position, he had the task of sentencing Jews who were found to be practicing their religion. He was known as a harsh judge who did not hesitate to condemn to death any Jew who refused to convert.

One day, an elderly Jew wrapped in his *tallis* and *tefillin* was brought before this judge. The judge sentenced him to death, and began to sign the decree. However, his hand would not budge. It seemed to have lost its power. He tried again, and still his hand would not move. He tried several more times to lift his hand, but it would not obey his will.

Suddenly, inside his head, a thought screamed out, "Perhaps this is my father and that is why I can't sign the decree."

He ordered the elderly man to enter his private office, and sent his assistants away. "Did you ever have a son who was taken away from you by the church?" he asked the man.

"Yes," said the man sadly. "My Moshe. He was my son."

"Did he have any identifying marks on his body that would enable you to identify him?" the judge asked.

"Yes, he had two scars on his right shoulder," said the man.

At that, the judge's eyes instantly welled up with tears. "Father!" he shouted, and the two men fell on each other's shoulders crying with tears of joy. Shortly after this episode, Moshe escaped from the church and returned to his roots.

Rav Elyah would conclude this story with a message: The natural love and connection between a son and his father is so strong that even though many years had passed, and the boy had become hardened and ruthless toward his fellow Jews, these factors could not cause a rift between father and son. The connection could never be broken.

If that is the case between a man and his son, who are after all, only human, how much more indestructible is the connection between a Jew and his Father in Heaven. Even when we separate ourselves from Hashem with walls of steel, the love remains. You can see it in these boys who ran to make a *berachah*. You may have thought that, with no religion in their homes, they have completely forgotten their Father, but that is only temporary. As soon as the memory of their Father returns to them, they desire with all their heart to come close to Him.

Rav Zilberstein then related an event that took place in the Israeli city of Cholon a few years earlier. At that time, every day many missiles were hitting the city and keeping the inhabitants in a state of terror. A day of prayer and inspiration was organized in the center of the town, and residents from all quarters converged there, seeking some succor for their troubles.

A Sefer Torah was given a place of honor at the gathering. The people stood in line before the Torah, and one by one, each gave it a kiss. Jews of every type stood in that line and waited their turn to reverently, lovingly kiss the holy scroll. Even those who would not set foot in a synagogue knew instinctively that the Torah's soothing light could cut through the darkness of their situation. On that day, I realized that, indeed, no matter how far away a son may have drifted, he can never be separated from his loving Father in heaven.

A Jew's mission is to bring Hashem's holiness into our world. Even when our minds and hearts are looking elsewhere, our souls in-

stinctively look to Heaven, for that is where all that we truly want and need in life resides.

A Dream Come True

In the following story, Mrs. Chavie Bauman, a young mother living in Lakewood, N.J. gives a truly remarkable account of a chilling, yet most inspiring episode in her life. It sends us a clear message of emunah, teaching that there exists another world, where the only things that matters are Torah, mitzvos, and kedushah.

On Shabbos, *Parashas Vayeishev*, December 17, 2011, I finished my *seudah* with my family and went to my room for a most welcome Shabbos afternoon nap. I stretched out comfortably and, sleepy from the meal, fell into a deep sleep. In my dream state, a strange scenario unfolded. My brother, who is *baruch Hashem* alive and well, was standing with a saintly looking man whom I did not know. The man had a full black beard, long *peyos,* and the round hat of the Yerushalmi Jews.

Looking directly into my eyes, the man spoke to me in a manner that left no room for questions.

"You must learn the *sefer Oz Vehadar Levushah,*" he stated simply. The book, subtitled *Modesty — An Adornment for Life,* provides in great detail the rules regarding modesty for women, and relates much background material on the subject. I told the man that I could not learn that *sefer*. It was far too restrictive for women of my generation. But my saintly visitor wasn't hearing any objection. "You must learn *Oz Vehadar Levushah,*" he repeated. Then, he vanished.

My eyes sprang open and I could feel my heart beating hard, as if I had been running at top speed. What did this dream mean? It was so frighteningly vivid that I nearly expected to find the man standing right there in front of me.

After a while, however, I calmed down. The best idea, I thought, wasto try to forget about the dream. In my most honest self-appraisal, I simply did not feel that Oz *Vehadar Levushah* was for me. I certainly aspired to dress as modestly as I could, but that *sefer,* with its many guidelines and rules, simply seemed to me to be beyond my capability. Anyway, the entire episode was only a dream, so why was I spending so much time pondering the imaginary man's advice?

The next day, while visiting my parents, I recounted my dream to my mother. As I was telling her the details, my brother — the one who had appeared in the dream — strode into the kitchen where we were sitting. I told him that he had appeared in my dream on Shabbos afternoon, in the company of a *tzaddik* whom I could not identify. My brother's face turned ash white.

"What did the *tzaddik* look like?" he asked. "Describe every detail!"

As I painted a picture of the man, my brother's face registered increasing levels of disbelief. "I saw him too!" he shouted. "The same exact man came to me in my dream on Shabbos! I was in a *sefarim* store, and he came over to me and told me, 'You must strengthen your *limud haTorah.*' Then he pointed out a *sefer* he wanted me to learn. After that, he disappeared, and I woke up shaking."

The family agreed that this was no random occurrence. "This is like something from a tale of long ago," I remarked. "Things like this don't happen in our day and age!" Each of us pondered the mystery, but none of us had a clear idea of why this man had sought us out and delivered his messages.

That afternoon, my mother received an automated telephone call inviting Lakewood women to a special event scheduled for that evening at a local hall. Although neither my mother nor I usually went out to these events, my mother called and asked me to join her. Suddenly feeling the need for a night out of the house, I agreed.

Several hours later, we walked together through the entrance of the hall and were confronted by a table containing books that were being sold in conjunction with the event. When I read the title on the books, I drew a sharp breath of shock. Piles of Oz *Vahadar Levushah* lay there, staring me in the face. Struck by the clear Divine hand in our decision to attend this event, my mother immediately purchased a copy of the book. We took our seats, among a few hundred women in the community, to hear a presentation called "Daughters of Dignity," focusing on the topic of *tzenius*.

The messages from the Next World just kept getting louder. The first speaker, Mrs. Esther Bick, opened her remarks with the statement of Rav Yosef Chaim Sonnenfeld, who, shortly before his passing, proclaimed that the last *nisayon* before Mashiach comes will be in our approach to *tzenius*. On hearing this quote, my mother and I both began to cry, for Rav Yosef Chaim Sonnenfeld was my mother's great-great-grandfather. He had clearly reached into our world to guide my mother and me to this presentation.

Rav Yosef Chaim Sonnenfeld

Nevertheless, I had seen photographs of him and knew that he was not the man in my dream. With our hearts thus open and our ears now attentive to the message Heaven seemed so intent upon sending us, we absorbed the speakers' insights and found much inspiration in the event.

As the audience filed out of the hall to head home, my mother and I wove our way to the front in order to speak to Rebbetzin Klughaupt, the daughter of the holy Skulener Rebbe. We told her about the dream and the mysterious man and all the events in the past 24 hours. My mother asked her if she would relate the dream to her saintly father and seek out his advice on our behalf. The Rebbetzin, who was astounded by the dream, agreed to discuss it with her father and get back to us as soon as possible.

We waited anxiously to hear from the Rebbetzin, and at last, she called. The Rebbe's message was that the dream was real and its directive should be taken seriously. He informed us that the man who appeared in our dreams was without a doubt an ancestor.

As the Rebbetzin explained in her father's name, "People think that after a person passes from this world, he has nothing more to do with what is happening here. But that is not true. When parents and grandparents pass away, they maintain a strong bond with their descendants. They have great pleasure from their *limud haTorah* and from the mitzvos they perform. On the other hand, when we slacken in our *avodas Hashem,* our ancestors experience great distress.

The Rebbe's message was clear: "Take this dream to heart and begin to work on yourself accordingly." He added that we would be performing a further mitzvah by publicizing the dream.

Since the dream, my life, which I had always thought of as a "normal, ordinary life," has changed into something far more meaningful than I could have imagined. I took the message to heart as the Rebbe advised, and went through my wardrobe disposing of things that I felt might not meet the level of *tzenius* expected of me. I purchased new clothing and began a new campaign. Besides studying the laws of *tzenius* on my own, I began a group called "Peninim," a small gathering of women who meet twice a month to learn and discuss the laws and strengthen our approach to this mitzvah, all based on the *sefer Oz Vehadar Levushah.*

During the weeks following the dream, our family began to look through old pictures of our grandparents and great-grandparents, trying unsuccessfully to find the face of the man my brother and

I had seen. Then one day, my mother dug up a faded old picture that had been taken at least 60 years earlier. She showed it to my brother, and his eyes opened wide in amazement. "That's him! The man in my dream!" he declared with complete certainty.

Rav Shmuel Hillel Shenker

Without telling me that my brother had already identified the picture, my mother showed it to me. I could not believe my eyes, but there before me was the exact face, the same serious, saintly visage, that I had seen in my dream.

My mother told us that the man who had come to us was her great-grandfather, Rav Shmuel Hillel Shenker of Yerushalayim. He was the son of Rav Avrohom Shenker, the original founder of the Slabodka Yeshivah. Rav Shmuel Hillel was a highly regarded *mussar* personality, and the son-in-law of Rav Yosef Chaim Sonnenfeld.

What can a person possibly think when her revered great-grandfather comes from the World of Truth to give his great grandchildren *mussar*? People sometimes rationalize that they do not know what Hashem wants from them, but our ancestor, in his love for us, steered us clear of all rationalizations and set us on the track to eternity.

A few weeks after we found this photograph, my friend's husband told us that he had done some research and discovered that Rav Shmuel Hillel had written a *sefer* titled *Chochmas Lev* on the topic of *kedushah* and *tzenius*. Simultaneous with the publication of the *sefer*, he founded a organization called "Agudas HaKodesh," with the goal of promoting *kedushah*, *tzenius*, and *taharas Yisrael*. Now the entire puzzle was complete. Rav Shmuel Hillel had come to me because this was the mitzvah to which he had dedicated so much of his life; he wanted to ensure that his legacy lived on in his children. Still, I wondered why he had chosen an ordinary person like me, rather than a respected Rebbetzin, to receive his message. Then I realized that it was precisely because I was an ordinary person that I became the receptacle, for if I could overcome my resistance, others could do so as well.

I hope that my true story will awaken those woman who read it to the realization that *tzenius* is something we can all work on. Our efforts are a credit and a *nachas* to our holy ancestors who live in the World of Truth and see the falsehood of all the obstacles we perceive and imagine. And most importantly, the Father of us all will look with pride and pleasure at His beautiful daughters of dignity.

Mrs. Bauman teaches us that with the right inspiration and a clear, honest look at our lives, we really can ascend to levels we think are beyond us.

A Matter of Control

In a material world where it appears that actions lead to results, it is sometimes difficult to remember that Hashem is in control, and that all our success is a result of siyata d'Shmaya, the heavenly assistance that enables our efforts to bear fruit.

After weeks of heartbreaking helplessness, Rabbi Nosson Kauptman* finally dared to hope that his little son, Moshe, might finally be cured. Watching the child deal with so much pain was extremely difficult. But now, at last, father and son were heading down the corridor of the ICU toward the office of the renowned Dr. David Simmons,* one of Israel's top surgeons.

Reb Nosson clutched his *Tehillim* in one hand, and his son's small hand in the other. "Please, Hashem, please help my poor little boy. May this doctor be the *shaliach*!"

As the father and son entered Dr. Simmons' office and sat down across from him, he remained absorbed in Moshe's massive file of test reports and charts. Reb Nosson held his little boy tightly on his lap, trying to deliver by osmosis the courage and love the child needed.

At last, the doctor looked up and smiled. "Rabbi Kauptman, I am going to cure your little boy," he said confidently. "It's a delicate procedure, but you are fortunate in that you have come to one of the only surgeons in the world who is experienced in this area. I wouldn't trust it to anyone else in Israel, frankly. But I have looked over the x-rays and tests, and I am certain that this can be done. Go to my secretary before you leave, and she will schedule the operation."

Reb Nosson was filled with optimism for the first time in weeks. "Thank you, doctor!" he nearly shouted. "With Hashem's help, everything should go just as you say!"

Suddenly, Reb Nosson noticed that the doctor's face was turning from sunny confidence to cloudy turbulence.

"Hashem should help?" he repeated in a tone drenched with sarcasm. "Why are you getting G-d involved in this? I am the one in control, not G-d!"

Rabbi Kauptman could not believe what he was hearing. He knew that the doctor was not a religious Jew, but he could not understand how a man with Jewish blood pumping through his veins could speak in such a despicable way.

"Please take back what you just said!" demanded Rabbi Kauptman. "It won't do my son or you any good for you to talk in such a haughty manner."

The doctor's cold sarcasm boiled into a rage, and he began to spew forth words of outright hatred and heresy. He then banged on the table and repeated over and over, "I am the one in control here. I am the one in control here. Go find G-d back home in Bnei Brak. Here, I'm in control!"

Rabbi Kauptman grasped his son by the hand, turned around and marched out of the office, trembling with shock and anger at the doctor's words. As the days went by and the date of the operation approached, he could not shake the terrible recollection of the scene in Dr. Simmons' office. He worried about placing his son's life in the hands of such a man; could this doctor possibly merit the *siyata d'Shmaya* needed to perform this operation successfully?

Overwhelmed with confusion, Rabbi Kauptman paid a visit to Hagaon Rav Chaim Kanievsky. At the very least, he wished to get the *gadol's berachah* for his son's complete recovery. But more than that, he longed to unburden his soul.

As he related the story of Dr. Simmons' outburst to Rav Chaim, he saw the *gadol* recoil at the doctor's horrendous words. Nevertheless, Rav Chaim urged Rabbi Kauptman to put the matter out of his mind.

"Of course you were shocked to see the honor of Hashem being trampled on like that," said Rav Chaim. "But you need not worry about it. Allow Hashem to take care of this issue and you will see how it will all work out."

A few nights later, some time after midnight, Rabbi Kauptman was getting ready to retire for the night when the phone rang. Surprised by the late-night call, he quickly snatched up the phone.

"Rabbi Kauptman, is that you?" a voice on the other end asked pleadingly. "Is it you? This is Dr. Simmons."

Rabbi Kautpman had instantly recognized the voice.

"Yes, it's me. What's wrong, doctor?"

"Please, Rabbi Kauptman, let me take back what I said. I take it all back."

"Of course you can take it back ... what's the matter?"

"Well, you surely remember how I was screaming at you the

other day, telling you that I was the one in control. You pleaded with me to take back my foolish words and I refused."

Rabbi Kauptman could hardly believe the change in the doctor's tone. From a man whose arrogance had reached unheard of proportions, he had deflated into a humble, chastised penitent. "I do remember. In fact, it's hard for me to forget."

"Well, I can tell you today, without a doubt, that I am not the one in control! I am not in charge," the doctor declared. "Hashem is the One and only One in charge! I have no power of my own."

"I'm relieved to hear you saying this, Dr. Simmons. But what happened to change your mind?"

"The most humiliating thing that has every happened to me. I have never in my life experienced anything like it. You see, I had to give a presentation in front of a few hundred doctors at a major conference. I've done these presentations a million times, but this time, for no reason I can fathom, I became panic-stricken. My stomach was cramping and churning, and all of a sudden, I lost control of my bowels. Like a baby. I lost control. I quickly ended my speech and left the stage in shame.

"So there was Hashem, telling me loud and clear that I can't even control my own body without His help. Never mind controlling the operation and your son's recovery. Never mind controlling anything. It's all Hashem. It's only Hashem. And with Hashem's help, we will cure your child."

The doctor learned a difficult lesson, but Rabbi Kauptman learned something valuable, as well. When we stand up for the honor of Hashem, we will ultimately create a kiddush Hashem. We must do our part, and Hashem will do the rest. How foolishly we act when we fail to recognize this, and believe that everything rests on our own intelligence, strength, and effort.

The Maggid, Rav Sholom Schwadron, used to relate an amusing, but telling story to illustrate the folly of this thinking.

Many years ago, at the entrance to Yerushalayim, a man named Yankel used to stand all day directing traffic. He was not a traffic officer or a crossing guard, but he felt that the obligation to ensure the smooth and safe passage of cars into the city rested entirely on him.

The intersection had perfectly operational traffic lights, but this fact did not make Yankel feel any less obligated to perform his task. Each day, without fail, he would be at his post, raising his hand and screaming "Stop!" when the light turned red, and then waving the traffic onward when it turned green. Yankel believed with all his heart that he was really in control of the flow of traffic into Yerushalayim.

The obligation rested heavy upon him. In the high heat of the Middle-Eastern summer and the cold, wind-blown rain of winter, he manned his post heroically. Back home, he had a wife who staunchly believed in him. She would wake him up each morning calling, "Yankel, Yankel, it's time to get up. Yerushalyim is waiting for you!" She proudly did her part to support her husband's vital work, rising early each morning to prepare his breakfast and pack sandwiches and coffee to sustain him during his grueling vigil.

One day, Yankel came home wearing an expression of deep concern.

"What happened?" his wife asked him. "Did something go wrong today? Was there an accident?"

"No," he replied. "Everything went perfectly, like clockwork. But I don't know what's going to be tomorrow. I heard that the President of the United States is coming. Can you imagine all the traffic that's going to bring? And I have to be sure that everything goes just perfectly. There can't be any traffic jams and there can't be any accidents. I hope I can handle it!"

These were the worries that occupied Yankel's mind. Once in a while, someone would sidle up to him at his post and try to draw him into a conversation, seeking to discover what the man was thinking. However, the conscientious Yankel would never engage in such idle chatter while on the job. Didn't people realize, he wondered, that with just one moment of distraction, disaster could ensue?

One day, Yerushalayim was hit with a rare snowstorm. Unaccustomed to driving in such conditions, motorists stayed home and the streets were nearly empty. Nevertheless, Yankel stood at his post, swaddled in a bulky winter coat, scarf, and hat. Noticing that the stalwart guardian of the city was standing idle, a passerby named Moshe approached him to start a conversation.

"Good morning, Yankel, how are things going today?" Moshe asked.

"You see how it's going," Yankel replied morosely, like a man whose business deal has just gone sour. "There is no work for me to do today because of the snow on the ground."

"Tell me Yankel, is your work hard on you?"

"Are you kidding?" Yankel answered incredulously. "I never get to take a break. I am here six days a week from morning to night, and no one is even willing to fill in for me for a day so that I can get a little rest. Of course it is hard!"

"I see what you mean. You do work hard. But what is it exactly that you do? Can you explain it to me?"

Yankel smiled broadly as he lifted up his hand, displaying it as if it were a rare artifact.

"You see this hand of mine? With this hand, I control all of Yerushalayim. With a wave of my hand, people go. And when I lift it up, they all stop."

Moshe didn't want to deflate Yankel's pride in his work, but he felt compelled to ask him the next obvious question.

"Yankel, tell me, why do you think that the cars are going and stopping because of your hand? Is it possible that they stop and go because the traffic light turns red and green?"

"Are you kidding me?" Yankel exclaimed as he leaped up from the little stool upon which he rested at his post. "The opposite is true! Do you think people would be more likely to obey to a silly mechanical traffic light, or a living person?"

"Okay, so I have an idea," said Moshe. "Let's do an experiment. You stop directing the traffic and we will see if the cars stop on their own when the light turns red, and if they go when it turns green. Then we will know if it's you or the lights that are really directing the traffic."

Yankel looked at Moshe as if he had just suggested that they commit a murder. "What are you saying?" he shouted. "What will happen if there is a terrible accident while we are trying to take your silly test? Do you want that on your head? I surely don't!"

Rav Schwadron expounds, "We have to remember that as much as we think we are running the world, in heaven they are laughing at us saying, 'Don't think that you are running the world, for you are not in charge. You are not in charge of the world, not in charge of the city, nor are you in charge of the entrance of the city. Know that you are not even in charge of yourself.' "

> *We must do our hishtadlus and do our best, but the outcome of all our life's efforts rests with Hashem. When we trust Hashem to do His part, we are free to do ours, expending our time and energy doing the one thing Hashem desires that we do for ourselves — building a life of Torah, mitzvos, and maasim tovim.*

Achakeh Lo B'chol Yom ...

We are told that when a person reaches the Next World and is asked to give an accounting of his years on earth, he must an-

swer the question, "Did you hope and long for the coming of Mashiach?" For most of us, this is a hard question to answer. We hope for Mashiach — for a better world and the end to our sorrows, for the clear Presence of Hashem to be recognized by one and all. But still, do we really know what it means to live each day in expectation of Mashiach's arrival?

Like the Chofetz Chaim before him, Rav Nosson Wachtfogel, the Lakewood *Mashgiach*, kept a bag packed. Any moment, any day, Mashiach would be here, and the great *tzaddik* wanted to be ready. It was that pure *emunah* that shone in the *Mashgiach's* eyes and saturated his words, bringing inspiration to his thousands of *talmidim* throughout the decades.

To him, Mashiach was not a dream. It was not a fuzzy, futuristic possibility. It was tomorrow's news. Just as people might stock up on water in anticipation of a storm, the *Mashgiach* sent a *talmid* every year before Pesach to reserve a sheep for him. He wanted to have a *korban pesach* ready when Mashiach arrived.

Rav Nosson dancing at a wedding to "Achakah Lo"

With that longing and eager anticipation burning in his heart, Rav Nosson was especially inspired by the song *"Achakeh Lo."* The words of this song are from the Jewish article of faith that states: "I believe with perfect faith in the coming of Mashiach, and even though he may tarry, I wait for him *(achakeh lo)* every day." This was Rav Nosson's "theme song." When he entered a wedding hall, the band would break into this tune, and the frail, elderly *Mashgiach* would jump to life, dancing and swaying to the words that touched his soul.

As he grew older, the obligations of his ever-productive life became more difficult to fulfill, and yet, his inner strength drove him to achieve what seemed super-human in others' eyes. In one of the last years of his life, the *Mashgiach* traveled to Eretz Yisrael to meet with *gedolim* and discuss the pressing issues of the times. After a long, exhausting day, he arrived for Maariv at the Yerushalayim shul known as Zichron Moshe, a place where a *minyan* could be found around the clock. It was midnight when the *Mashgiach* entered, flanked by his grandson and a few close *talmidim,* who guided his shaky steps.

Rabbi Tuvia Steinharter, who had also come for Maariv, caught sight of the *Mashgiach* and his small entourage. He was awed by the sight of this frail, elderly man pushing himself to the limit of his strength so that he could daven Maariv with a *minyan*. Reb Tuvia walked over to one of the *Mashgiach's* grandchildren, with whom he was acquainted.

"It's unbelievable to see the *Mashgiach's mesirus nefesh* to come and daven with a *minyan,*" Reb Tuvia told the grandson.

"If you think this is unbelievable," the grandson said, "you should have seen what happened last night!" He then told Reb Tuvia this story:

"It was 1 in the morning. My *zeide* was completely drained. He had been traveling around all day, sitting in long meetings, using up every bit of his strength. When he got home, he sat down on the sofa to rest. It got later and later, but he was too exhausted to pick himself up to go to bed. When I suggested that he get into bed and get comfortable, he looked up from his place on the sofa and said, 'I have no strength. Let me stay here for the night.'

"My cousin was with me, and we were both begging him, 'Please, *Zeide*, you need your rest. We'll help you get into bed.'

"We tried to lift him, but we couldn't manage it. He was so exhausted, he couldn't support even a little of his own weight.

"I wasn't sure what to do. We couldn't simply leave him there for the night, but on the other hand, there was no way to lift him onto his feet. Then all of a sudden, an idea flashed through my mind.

"I started singing, *achakeh lo ... achakeh lo* ... I sang his favorite *niggun* and clapped my hands, hoping to get him going. When my *zeide* heard the song, he suddenly came to life. His arms began to move and he started to clap. Then he began to sing, *V'af al pi sheyismame'ah im kol zeh achakeh lo ...*

"You could just see the energy surging through my *zeide's* blood, and he seemed to forget about his exhaustion. All of a sudden, without any help, he stood up and began to dance. We quickly grabbed hold of his hands and began to dance him across the apartment until we reached his bed. It was a sight to behold. A frail man, who did not even have the strength to move, was up on his feet, dancing across the room. His hope and yearning for the final redemption fueled his spirit."

When our yearning for Mashiach comes from deep emunah — the certainty that redemption can come at any moment — then it has the power to transform the way we live. Then we will not have to think hard to give our answer in the Next World, for our deeds in this world will answer for us.

A Child's Prayer

The purity of a child's prayers has the ability to open the gates of heavenly mercy. We can learn a lot from their simple way of speaking from their heart to Hashem, knowing that He is listening and will answer their plea

Moshe Kornfeld* had enough of hiding. All of Eretz Yisrael was in a state of high alert as Iraqi Scud missiles rained down onto civilian streets and sent people scrambling into bomb shelters and safe rooms. Air-tight room sealers and gas masks were distributed in anticipation of chemical warfare. Businesses and schools were closed, and everyone stayed in their homes, not knowing when the next missile would fall. Somehow, in the Gulf War of 1991, fought by America against Iraq, the entire nation of Israel had become the hostage.

Despite the dangers, Moshe Kornfeld wanted nothing more than to walk into his local *beis midrash* and learn as he had been doing all his life. He stepped out the door of his home feeling like a freed prisoner. It was a short walk on the deserted street to his shul in Ramat Elchonon.

The hour was late and the shul seemed deserted as he walked inside. Then his ears picked up a soft sound. It was a voice — a young boy's voice — and he sounded as if he were crying. Moshe peeked around the corner to where the *aron kodesh* stood, and there he saw a sight that represented to him the epitome of simple faith.

A young boy of about 8 was standing at the *bimah*, unaware of Moshe's presence. The boy was having an emotion-filled conversation with his Father in Heaven, in which he pleaded for all that was most important to him. In a voice choked with tears, he spoke these words:

Father in Heaven! You know that I believe that whatever You do is for our good, but please hear my prayer. I so badly want to go to cheder (school) to learn Torah, so why can't You get rid of that evil man in Iraq so that I can learn Torah again?

Father, I promise that if You do not take care of Saddam, then I will have to do so myself. How long can I hold myself back from going to cheder? You know that whenever I have free time, I go directly to a beis midrash to learn Torah and I don't busy myself with anything else. But how can I learn Torah now when I am so afraid?

Why do You punish the Jewish people so harshly? We all try our best to see the righteousness of Your actions, but if You continue to punish us then we will not have any more strength to handle it, and who will gain from that? No one. It wouldn't be good for us and it wouldn't be good for You either, so why do You continue to allow this evil man to harm us?

Father, I love my rebbi in cheder so much. I want to see him so badly. How much longer can I stay locked up in my house?

As the boy concluded his prayer, he burst into tears. Never in his life had Moshe seen such a beautiful prayer said with such purity of heart. Never would he forget what he saw.

Perhaps, in the merit of this young boy's prayer, Saddam's army was quickly defeated during the Gulf War. The power of a child's tefillah or his Torah study can protect Klal Yisrael from our enemies, as we learn in the following story:

The great *gadol hador,* Rav Yosef Shalom Elyashiv, had just finished delivering a *shiur*. A crowd followed him out to his car and stood around him, asking him questions as he prepared to leave. Suddenly, a young boy pushed through the crowd, jumped into the car and sat himself down right next to Rav Elyashiv. "I have a question to ask the Rav," the child said.

Rav Yosef Shalom Elyashiv

"Do you already know this week's *parashah* so well that you have other questions to ask?" Rav Elyashiv replied with a smile.

With full confidence, the boy said, "Yes!"

"All right then, let me ask you a question first," said the Rav. "It says in *Rashi* in *Parashas Vayetzei* (31:10) that angels would come and take the sheep that belonged to Lavan, and bring them over to become part of Yaakov's flock. Why wasn't Yaakov concerned that he had *gezel akum* (stolen property of a non-Jew)?"

The boy answered cleverly. "Once the angels grab hold of the sheep and have the power to do whatever they want with them, then these sheep are considered similar to the case of *zuto shel Yam* — a situation described in the Gemara in *Bava Metzia*, when rushing waters wash your property away and you give up hope of getting it back. The halachah is that whoever finds that property can keep it. Here, too, Yaakov was allowed to keep the sheep because once the angels took them, Lavan had certainly given up hope of getting them back. Then they are considered abandoned property that the finder can keep. Therefore, Yaakov had no concern of it being considered stolen property."

The boy's clever answer brought a broad smile to Rav Elyashiv's face. The next day at the daily *shiur*, Rav Elyashiv related the young boy's answer to his question. "Such a boy has the power, through the strength of his Torah learning, to destroy any atom bomb Iran would try to create to harm us," said the Rav. "With his Torah, he can literally overturn the entire world."

Yossi Shine* was a second-grader in a yeshivah in Lakewood. He was visiting Brooklyn for Shabbos and was eating his meal at the home of the Schechters,* close friends of the family. Bubby Schechter was there as well; she was an elderly woman who was adored by her grandchildren, and Yossi, too, felt very close to her.

During the Shabbos day meal, Bubby Schechter took ill. The worried family called Hatzolah right away, and after a quick check of her symptoms, the EMTs determined that she should be taken to the emergency room. The family, Yossi included, felt miserable thinking of poor Bubby lying sick in the hospital. Yossi wished he could help her, but what could a boy his age do?

After Shabbos, Yossi returned to Lakewood with his family. The moment that he arrived home, he bounded up the stairs to his room. A few minutes later, he came back downstairs holding a bag filled with change.

"What's this all about, Yossi?" his mother asked.

"This is the money I have been collecting this year," he explained proudly. "I have $4.25 in change. Is it possible that I can have 75 cents from you, Mommy?"

"Sure, Yossi. What do you need it for?"

"Oh, I just need $5 for yeshivah tomorrow," he answered mysteriously. "I will tell you about it when I come home." Yossi's mother gave him 75 cents and Yossi went to sleep happy.

The next day, when Yossi came home from yeshivah, he announced, "Mommy, Bubby Schechter will be coming out of the hospital today!"

"Well, Yossi, I hope you're right, but how do you know that?"

"Because every day in yeshivah, we say *Tehillim*, and if you bring in $5 for *tzedakah,* you are allowed to give in a name, and they say

Tehillim that day for the name you gave. I took the money that I saved up all year and put it together with the money you gave me, and today we were able to say *Tehillim* for Bubby Schechter. So I know for sure that she will be better and will leave the hospital today."

And just as Yossi said, Bubby Schechter was released from the hospital with a clean bill of health. That is the simple power of a *tefillah* produced by a heart filled with *emunah*. It's the power of a child's prayers.

A story is told about Rabbi Yeshayah Bardaki, one of the closest students of the Vilna Gaon. Rav Yeshayah was traveling to Eretz Yisrael on a ship when a huge storm set in. The ship was tossed violently from side to side as it neared Eretz Yisrael. Rav Yeshayah feared that the ship wouldn't be able to hold out much longer, and unfortunately, he was right. A terrifying cracking sound was heard as the ship began to fall apart. It quickly filled with water and capsized.

Rav Yeshayah fell into the raging water with his two children, a son and a daughter. He tried valiantly to keep them both afloat by swimming with them as they held onto his back, but after a while he realized that he would not be able to save both of them from drowning. He would have to choose which child to save, or his strength would give out and all of them would drown. It was a wrenching decision for a father to make, but it had to be done. He decided that he would save his son.

His heart raged as wildly as the water as he told his daughter that he would have to let her go, for he had no more strength to go on with both of the children. His daughter began to scream in fear.

"No, Tatty! You can't let go of me! I can't swim!" she pleaded.

Her grip tightened on her father's shoulder and she clung to him with every shred of her strength. Again Rav Yeshayah told her that, if she continued to hold on, they would all go down together. The little girl began to scream.

"Tatty! Tatty! You can't leave me. I have no other father but you!"

When Rav Yeshayah heard those words, a surge of energy flowed within him. He could not bear to see his daughter drown. With renewed strength, he grabbed hold of his daughter and began to swim as fast as he could toward shore. He didn't know how he would make it, but he knew he had to do it. With his last bit of strength, he made it safely to shore, where he and his two children collapsed, exhausted but alive.

He turned to his little girl and said, "My daughter, you know that when I said I had no more strength to carry you, I truly did not believe I could make it. But when you screamed out to me, 'Tatty, I have no other father but you,' the complete faith you put in me gave me new strength, and I was able to help you.

"For the rest of your life, I want you to remember what happened today, and anytime you find yourself in distress, don't give up hope. Rather, turn to Hashem and plead, 'Tatty, Tatty, I have no other Father but You. Please save me!' I am confident that you will be saved, because just as I could not leave you, your Father in heaven will not be able to leave you. He will save not only you, but the entire world as well."

The united heart of Klal Yisrael beat as one, desperately praying and hoping for the rescue of a lost little boy named Leiby Kletsky. Searchers by the thousands scoured the streets of Brooklyn day and night, searching for any hint of the child's whereabouts. When the news broke of the horrible tragedy that had taken Leiby's life, Klal Yisrael was plunged into shock and mourning. Eulogies and speeches resounded throughout the community as our leaders struggled to soothe the aching heart of a nation. During one of those gatherings, Rabbi Moshe Tuvia Lieff related a powerful vignette about Leiby:

Leiby was a boy who loved to daven. Watching him daven, you could see his love and joy for *tefillah,* as he never took his eyes off his *siddur.* One day after davening, his *zeide,* who was with him, said, "Leiby, you davened so beautifully today. How do you manage to have such concentration?"

"My rebbi taught us that every word we say with *kavanah* creates a *malach,* so I want to create lots of *malachim,*" he answered simply.

"But Leiby, how do you know that the *malach* you created is a healthy *malach.* Maybe it's a *tzuklapte malach,* an unhealthy one, one that is limping?"

Leiby replied, "*Zeide,* if you *daven* with *kavanah,* you know for sure that you created healthy *malachim.*"

Leiby believed in tefillah. He believed that we can create millions of malachim with our tefillos. We, too, must believe in the power of tefillah to create thousands of malachim who will protect us in times of trouble. Such tefillos will bring berachah to ourselves and to Klal Yisrael. And, they are a powerful zechus for Leiby, who is surely davening by the Heavenly Throne to bring an end to our bitter galus.

Chapter 2:

Teshuvah With All Your Heart

A Real Masterpiece

Besides his work as a kiruv rabbi, Rabbi Benzion Klatzko's other area of expertise is Jewish art. His home is decorated with many beautiful Jewish themed paintings. When he shared with me this story that combined art with kiruv, I knew we had a real masterpiece of a story to tell:

It was the day of Hoshana Rabbah, and I was at home with my family preparing for the last days of Yom Tov. A man named Shalom Goldberg was on his way over, having tracked me down as the owner of a painting created by his father, the artist Chaim Goldberg. The younger Goldberg was en route from Upstate New York to Florida, and would make a stop at my house on his way.

To fully appreciate what happened next, one needs a little background on the artist. There was a small *shtetl* in Poland called Kazimierz. In the 1930's, Kazimierz had a very small Jewish community, and among them was a righteous Jew named Shalom Goldberg. He and his wife shared their two-room house — really more of a hut — with their eight daughters and one son, Chaim. One room was the parents' bedroom, and the other room was an all-purpose space that served as the children's bedroom, the kitchen, and a shoe-repair shop, where Shalom earned his *parnassah*.

One day, a secularized Jew named Sol Steinberg was traveling through the town as part of his research on *shtetl* life. His interest, as an enlightened soul, was that of a historian, for he felt that he was recording the last throes of a dying way of life. Soon, he was sure, the Jewish people would abandon their superstitions and join the "modern" world.

Painting of Simchas Torah in Kazimierz, by Chaim Goldberg

Sol was walking through the streets of Kazimierz when he suddenly felt a sharp object pierce the the sole of his shoe. He asked the townspeople if they had a shoemaker in town and they told him to go to the home of Shalom Goldberg. The shoemaker greeted him graciously and invited him to sit down and wait while the repairs were made.

Sol looked around the simple home and noticed that its walls were adorned with some striking artwork. Small, intricately executed paintings and drawings portrayed moving scenes of a shul, a woman lighting Shabbos candles, and other depictions of Jewish life.

"Who made these beautiful paintings?" Sol asked Shalom. "They are absolutely stunning!"

"Oh, these drawings were made by my son Chaim," Shalom stated matter-of-factly.

"How old is your son?" Sol inquired.

"My son is 11 years old," the father answered.

"What? An 11-year-old boy made these beautiful paintings? He must be a genius. I must meet your son!" Sol insisted.

Shalom explained that Chaim was out working at his job as a house painter. He invited Sol to wait for his son to return home, and in his desire to meet the young artist, Sol gladly agreed to stay put.

When Chaim came home later that day, Sol was there to greet him.

"Did you really make those paintings yourself?" Sol asked the boy.

Chaim confirmed that he was the artist.

"These are some of the most impressive paintings I have ever seen," he told Chaim. "Let me see what else you've done." When Chaim was finished showing Sol his other work, the older man was nearly bursting with a passion to save him from obscurity.

"A boy with your talent doesn't belong in Kazimierz," he insisted. "I want you to come with me to Vienna and there you can join an art school and cultivate your talent. Your art will light up the world. You will become famous and wealthy. Come with me, for your own good and for the good of your people."

Chaim dismissed the idea instantly. His family counted on the money he earned painting houses. He could never leave them in poverty while he went to seek his fortune in Vienna. But Sol took his argument to Shalom, explaining that his son's talents should not be wasted. "He will have tremendous opportunities to make a wonderful living as an artist, and give himself and his family a better life," Sol argued.

Shalom, in his simplicity, did not understand what the enlightenment was about. He did not realize what it would mean to Chaim's spiritual life if Sol took him to Vienna. In his unselfish fatherly heart, he just wanted to give his son the opportunity for a better life. He agreed to send Chaim off with Sol, who brought him straight to one of Vienna's best art academies and marched him into the headmaster's office.

"Who do we have here?" the headmaster asked haughtily as he stared down at the young boy in tattered clothing. "I don't think this is the place for him."

Sol responded. "You have here a boy of enormous talent, unusual talent," he declared. "You do not want to pass up such a student."

"Well, then, let me see what he can do." The headmaster handed Chaim a chunk of plaster and told him to make something out of it. Chaim's deft hands worked the material until a small, lovely statue of a young girl emerged.

"Buy him some clothing and bring him back tomorrow to begin classes," the headmaster told Sol. Thus began Chaim's formal art education.

Meanwhile, Sol continued his quest to promote Chaim's career. He gathered up Chaim's paintings and brought them to Paris, where he showed them to one of the era's foremost artists, Marc Chagall. (Many people today are acquainted with Chagall as the creator of the twelve stained glass windows that depict each of the twelve tribes. His works — mostly of Jewish themes — are internationally recognized and prized.)

The instant Chagall saw Chaim's paintings, he knew he was viewing the work of an artistic genius. When he found out that the artist was only a child, he was even more convinced that a new prodigy had been discovered. "I will buy fifty-two of this boy's paintings right now," said Chagall. "Certainly he will be famous one day, and I want to own his work."

Chaim stayed in the school in Vienna for a few years, and then the war broke out. He was eventually captured by the Russians and sent to Siberia, where he remained for the duration of the war. When peace came, he resumed the pursuit of his passion. Chaim Goldberg's fame did indeed spread, as his mentor had predicted. His stunning depictions of *shtetl* life, drawn from the memories of his youth, hang in the most prestigious museums and galleries in the world.

Now, to resume the story … Shalom Goldberg, the son of Chaim, arrived at our house shortly before our Hoshana Rabbah meal. I invited him in and we spoke for the next half hour about his father and himself. Then I asked him, "By the way, where is your wife? You said you were traveling with her to Florida."

"She's in the car waiting for me," he replied.

"It's hot outside," I told him. "Please invite her in for a cold drink."

"No, no, she's fine. Anyway, she only drinks diet Cherry Doctor Pepper."

"Unbelievable. That happens to be my favorite drink, too," I told him. "I've got a fridge full of it. Please invite her in."

He went to his car and returned with his wife. Sitting at the table over our cold sodas, we began to talk about various subjects. Then I brought up the fact that today was Hoshana Rabbah, and I explained to him that it was an important day that shared certain themes with Yom Kippur.

"It also happens to be the last day we can shake the *lulav*," I added. "Hey, would you like to do it? I have a *lulav* and *esrog* right here that you could use."

"Rabbi, I don't know anything about a *lulav* and *esrog*," he said, as if this disqualified him from doing the mitzvah. "I go to shul on Rosh Hashanah and Yom Kippur, and that's pretty much it for Judaism … but you know what, we're here anyway, so why not?"

I guided him through the *berachah* and the mitzvah, noticing that both he and his wife seemed touched by their contact with this piece of their ancient heritage. So I took the next logical step.

"You know, luckily you also happened to show up right before our Hoshana Rabbah meal. You must be hungry, so why don't you stay. We have pastrami and corn beef on kosher rye, with pickles and mustard — the whole deal. You'll love it!"

Shalom looked a little uncomfortable and started making moves to leave, but his wife spoke up. "You know, that really sounds good. I think we'll stay."

They sat down with us and we had a very enjoyable lunch together. After the meal, I offered to take Shalom to the home of one of my neighbors, who was a great art-lover and had an impressive collection. That visit lasted several hours, and by the time we got back to my house, Shemini Atzeres was just a few hours away.

I described the oncoming Yom Tov celebration to Shalom and his wife and invited them to stay for the meal. Challah, gefilte fish, chicken soup with kreplach, sweet-and-sour chicken — it sounded too tempting to pass up, and so they accepted my invitation.

Our table was packed with guests that night, and Shalom and his wife were enjoying every minute of it. We sang songs, and I made sure to include some that Shalom would know. He began to sing along, his face aglow with happiness. As a prelude to Simchas Torah, we got up and began to dance around the table. Shalom shouted to me, in wonder and delight, "You know, Rabbi, the *shtetl* isn't dead!"

"Right!" I replied. "It just moved to Monsey!"

I let the meal move along slowly, with plenty of conversation and singing, in part because I was hoping to finish so late that Shalom and his wife would agree to stay the night. When we finally finished our tea and cake, it was already 11:30 p.m.

"Oh, my, look at how late it is," said Shalom as he checked his watch. "We really have to hit the road!"

"Can I run something by you?" I asked. "I have a clean, empty bedroom that you are welcome to use for the night if you would like."

"Thank you very much, Rabbi," he answered, "but we are on our way to Florida and we have a long trip ahead of us. I think we had better get going."

"Sure, but you're going to have to stop somewhere to sleep anyway. Why pay $80 for a motel room a couple of hours from now when you can have a free place to stay right now?"

Shalom's wife saw my point. "We might as well save ourselves the $80," she told her husband. And so, they stayed.

The next morning, we made a *minyan* in my home. I didn't wake up Shalom for davening, as I didn't want to disturb him. But when we reached *Yizkor* I assumed that Shalom would probably want to participate. I knocked on his door and told him that we would be praying *Yizkor* shortly. "Maybe you would like to say it in memory of your father?" I suggested.

"I would love to come join you," he said. "I just need a few minutes to get ready."

Soon Shalom came into the room where we were davening. He approached me and said in a half-whisper, "Rabbi, I don't have a *tallis*." I quickly got him one of the many extras I keep on hand. He wrapped himself up in it and he began to sway back and forth to the sounds of others' *tefillos* and those of his own heart. I left the room for the *Yizkor* prayer, as is the tradition for those who are blessed with two living parents.

A few minutes later, *Yizkor* was over and Shalom emerged from the room. I saw that his eyes were glistening with the remnants of tears as he strode purposefully to where I was standing and wrapped me in a warm hug.

"Rabbi, I can't explain it but I just feel that my father wanted me to be here today," he said. "He wanted me to feel what life in the *shtetl* was all about, what I was missing all these years. I feel that my father was the one who guided me to your home to send me this message."

"You have no idea how right you are," I told him. "Come with me for a minute."

I brought him to the spot where his father's painting was hanging. "Take a good look at the scene in the picture," I urged. "Do you realize that this is a painting of Simchas Torah in Kazimierz? That is the one painting of your father that we own. He was sending you the clearest message that you could ever imagine!"

I pointed out the details of the scene in Kazimierz. The men were dancing around the *bimah* with their small children riding their backs or borne in their arms. The excited children waved flags and the women looked upon the scene from a balcony. The warmth and joy, the sense of community, the love of family and of Torah literally leapt off the canvas into the viewer's heart.

"You see what the enlightenment did to people, Shalom? It pulled them away from all of this and filled them up with doubts, so that in the end, all they have of this beautiful heritage are paintings of the old days. They think that the happiness in those paintings no longer exists, but it does. It's alive in America right now, for people who still live their lives with the Torah."

Shalom was overjoyed at his discovery of the "living *shtetl.*" He promised me that he would return to my home soon and continue his journey to reclaim a world that he had thought was in the past, but was in reality the key to his future.

It was known that the enlightenment movement had also tried to recruit another boy, a genius named Arke Sislovitzer. Arke had the potential to become a great mathematician in a university, yet, baruch Hashem, at the tender age of 13, he enrolled in the yeshivah in Slabodka. He became known to the world as the great Rav Aharon Kotler, the man who would build Torah in America and create an impact that is felt throughout the world.

The story of Chaim Goldberg is a story of the choices made when we reach a crossroads in life. Rabbi Ephraim Wachsman told a powerful story on the same theme a few years ago when he spoke to a large group of boys in camp.

Expounding on the phrase from the mishnah in Sanhedrin (recited as an introduction to Pirkei Avos each week) that says, "Kol Yisrael yeish lahem chelek L'Olam Haba" (Every person in Klal Yisrael has a portion in the World to Come), he said that beyond the simple meaning, the verse teaches that "Every person in Klal Yisrael has a portion (chelek) that no one else in the world has or will ever have for the rest of eternity."

He explained his thoughts with a parable:

There was a poor farmer boy whose father put him to work caring for the cattle and the sheep. Each morning he would milk the cows and take the animals out to the fields to graze. As he sat high in the mountains keeping a watchful eye on his flock, he would pass the time by singing beautiful songs.

One day, a passerby on the road overheard the boy's singing. Entranced by the beauty of his voice, he climbed to the spot where the boy was sitting and greeted him. "My child," he said, "what are you doing here on this farm? You have such a wonderful voice! You could be making millions of dollars and delighting the world with such a special voice!"

The boy was clearly flattered, but could not believe that his talent was at all extraordinary. Nevertheless, the man persisted with his visions for the boy's future. "Let's go talk to your father about this," he suggested.

The boy and the man left the fields and found the boy's father. The man explained that he was certain that this boy could become a great singer whose voice would inspire the world.

"This isn't for us," the father said firmly. "He's got a nice voice, but so what? I'm a farmer, my father was a farmer, and his father was a farmer. Now my son has learned to be a farmer. He belongs here with me."

The man insisted that such talent shouldn't be wasted. "You don't have to believe me," he told the father. "I have a friend who is one of the greatest names in music. Come with me to see him and we will let him judge your son's talent."

After some cajoling, the father agreed. They brought the boy to the musician, who asked the boy to sing his favorite song. For a few minutes, the room filled up with the sweetest, most melodious sounds the musician had ever heard. Then the song came to an end.

"My boy, you have the most beautiful voice I have ever heard in my entire life! I have heard hundreds of singers but none with a voice equal to yours. Not only that, but I believe there has never been a boy with such a voice, and I don't believe there ever will be another like you. You are going to be very rich and famous one day."

The father, who until now had remained silent, cried out "Enough! I have heard enough of this talk about singing. Come son, we are leaving."

"But sir, don't you realize what a talent you have here?" the musician pleaded. "You are not just depriving him, you are depriving the world!"

"I have made up my mind. My grandfather was a farmer, my father was a farmer, and I am a farmer. My son is a farmer and that is what he will remain."

> *Each of us has greatness inside. Each neshamah is sent into this world with the talents and skills it needs to create its own masterpiece of Torah and mitzvos. The tragedy is when, like the singer, we do not seek the opportunity to develop the gifts Hashem has given us. For if we don't do it, who will?*

A few years ago, the great *Mashgiach* from Eretz Yisrael, Rav Don Segal, visited America and addressed a group of high school boys who were struggling with their *Yiddishkeit.* He spoke encouragingly to them, telling them that they each had the potential to become great in the world of Torah if they made the effort to do so. To illustrate his point, he related a short story about Rav Aharon Kotler.

Years ago, on a visit to Eretz Yisrael, Rav Aharon gave *shiurim* in various locations around the country. One day, he came to a kibbutz to give a *shiur*. Among those in the *shiur* was a young boy who lived on the kibbutz. At one point, this boy raised his hand to ask Rav Aharon a question. Rav Aharon responded, "That is a very good question." Turning to the young boy, he asked, "Do you go to yeshivah?"

The boy told him that he did not attend yeshivah.

"A boy who asks such good questions belongs in a yeshivah," Rav Aharon said.

Rav Aharon's words motivated this boy to insist that his parents send him to yeshivah to learn Torah.

"Do you know who that young boy on the kibbutz was?" Rav Segal asked the high-school boys he was addressing. "That boy was me. Rav Aharon saw that I had great potential, and the truth is, we all have great potential. We just have to make the effort to tap into that potential and then we can achieve great things in life."

The Royal Family

The children of the king are ever conscious of their noble heritage. They talk and walk, dress, and treat others with a dignity and grace befitting their station. The royal family knows that the image they project reflects on the king himself, and thus, they are careful to avoid anything that appears common and vulgar. And although they must maintain a higher standard than others, they also enjoy an unmatched benefit: they are beloved, supported, and protected by the most powerful figure in the land. They are special to him.

Dina Moyler* sat in the doctor's office waiting for the verdict. After weeks of crippling headaches that no aspirin could defeat, Dina Moyler finally made an appointment with a specialist in Manhattan. Hearing her complaints, the doctor sent her immediately to undergo an MRI, which would produce precise images of her brain. Now, she waited nervously to learn what the doctor saw in those images.

The expression he wore as he entered the office telegraphed immediately a dire message. "The images did reveal the source of your headaches, Mrs. Moyler," he told her. "The situation is rather serious. If you would like, you could come back with your husband and I could discuss it with both of you together."

Dina could not walk out of the office without a definitive diagnosis. She would have to handle whatever the news was on her own. "No, I don't want to wait for my husband," she announced. "I would like to hear everything now."

The doctor hung the MRI image in front of a light box on the wall. He pointed out a large, darkened area that extended from her ear into the interior section of her brain. "There is no easy way to tell you this," said the doctor. "You have a very unfortunate situation." He outlined the darkened area of the MRI with his finger. "This area here is a tumor," he told her. "It is about the size of a softball."

"So I'm going to need brain surgery?" Dina asked fearfully.

"I very much wish that we could offer you brain surgery," the doctor said. "But the fact is that the size and position of the tumor makes it inoperable."

"What does that mean?" Dina asked, a sense of panic rising inside her chest. "What's going to happen?"

"Well, Mrs. Moyler, no one can say exactly what is going to happen," the doctor replied, trying to inject at least a little hope into a hopeless situation. "But in the normal course of events, I'm so sorry to tell you, such a tumor is a terminal condition."

"You mean I'm going to die?" Dina nearly choked on the word. "How long? How long will I live?"

"Once again, that's not something I could state with certainty," the doctor said gently. "But based on my experience, I would say about three months." There was a moment of silence, and then the doctor left the office, providing his bereft patient some time to digest the information in private.

"Three months!" Dina repeated, the shock of the situation making her feel as though she were an onlooker in someone else's life drama. But no, it was her life, and it was almost over. Her heart felt as though it would explode with emotion. Tears began to cascade down her cheeks and she collapsed into weeping. Like an arrow through the air, the years of her life flashed before her eyes. What had she accomplished? How many silly, meaningless little concerns had occupied her days? "No, Hashem," she thought. "I'm not done yet! I can do so much better. Please give me time, and I will live as I should. I will live as Your daughter should!"

At that moment, Dina thought of all the corners she had cut in her service to Hashem. Well, those days were over. She would dress with modesty as her first priority. She would encourage her husband and sons in their Torah learning. She would gently and firmly raise the standards of mitzvah observance in her home. From now on, she thought, she would live with an eye to pleasing her Father in Heaven in every way possible. Perhaps then He would see how much His precious daughter wanted to serve Him in this world, and give her a new lease on life.

After about five minutes, the doctor re-entered the office. "What would you like to do?" he asked her. "I don't really see any worthwhile options for you."

Dina composed herself. "But I do see an option," she told the doctor.

"Really? What is it?" the doctor asked.

Pointing toward heaven, she answered, "G-d will help me. I know that He will. He has to, because I am His daughter and a Father takes care of His daughter."

"I am really impressed with your faith," the doctor responded sincerely. "I have a number of patients who would really benefit from that kind of faith, because from a medical perspective there is not much I can do for them."

"Well, doctor, faith is the only thing that is going to get me through this," Dina answered. "It's in G-d's hands. And the truth is, even if you could treat me, it would still be in G-d's hands. The only difference is that now, I can't pretend that there are other factors."

Dina left the office lost in her thoughts. Today was one of those red-letter days that divides one's life into "before" and "after." She didn't know how she was going to deal with this sickness, but at the same time she found strength in her conviction that Hashem could do anything.

Dina got on the subway to head back to her home in Brooklyn. A few minutes into her ride, she realized that she had gotten onto the wrong train and was heading in the opposite direction. Her overwrought nerves now surged with panic. Her little boy would be getting off his schoolbus on the busy street called Ocean Parkway, and she would not be there to meet him! He would be so frightened, and perhaps a stranger would approach him. What could she do?

Overwhelmed with anxiety that seemed to be rising up from every corner of her life, Dina broke down in tears right there on the subway. "Hashem, help me!" she cried. "I am a *Bas Melech* and You have to take care of me."

She jumped off the train at the next stop and ran to the other side of platform, where she caught the train to Brooklyn. As soon as she got home, she called the school office. The bus driver had returned her son to school when he saw that there was no adult waiting to greet him at his stop.

"I hate to ask you this favor," she said to the school secretary. "But could someone there please bring my son home? I've had a very hard day, and I don't know how long it will take me to get over there."

"We'll see if we can get him a ride," the secretary said. "We'll call you back as soon as we know." Dina hung up the phone and burst into a fresh torrent of tears.

"Hashem, where are You? I need You now. Please help me! Send me a sign that You are listening to me!"

At that moment, her cell phone began to buzz. Checking the screen, she saw that a text message had just arrived. It was a group message for a *shemiras halashon* group. It read: "The Chofetz Chaim says that *lashon hara* begins with the ear hearing the slanderous talk. Then those words extend to the mind, and then enter the soul. Hashem hates when someone speaks *lashon hara* so much that in the next world, the first thing Hashem punishes is the person's ears, then his mind, and then his soul."

When Dina read this message, her heart skipped a beat. She dropped the phone and began to scream, "Hashem, thank You! Thank You! You have answered me!"

Dina realized that she had received the prescription that would cure her sickness — a sickness that began in her ear, extended to her mind, and would eventually take her soul. The way to fight it, then, was to take upon herself a sharp focus on *shemiras halashon*, to purify her ears, her mind, and her soul.

That day, Dina began learning the *halachos* of *shemiras halashon*. She called Rabbi Duvi Bensoussan that night and told him that she wanted to join the *shemiras halashon* group that he ran in her shul. As a member of the group, she would receive a text message of a halachah from the Sefer Chofetz Chaim each night. She then told Rabbi Bensoussan the story and how the text message had come to her that very day as a clear sign from heaven.

Her story left one astonishing question unanswered. "But your number isn't on my list," said Rabbi Bensoussan. "How could you have gotten this text message today? It wasn't sent out to you. You aren't one of our subscribers!"

Dina couldn't answer. All she knew was that the message had come.

To this day, no one knows how Dina got that message, but it became very clear that the King was indeed taking care of His daughter. Since that text message, Dina has been learning the halachos of *shemiras halashon* every day. She has been watching her words, and Hashem has been watching over her. It has been two years since the doctor told her she had only three months to live. The doctors are baffled, because somehow, the tumor has been shrinking.

We, however, are not baffled. Hashem protects those who protect their mouth from speaking evil. When we speak and act with the dignity of the royal family, our King recognizes His beloved child and exercises His limitless power to save us from harm.

Our role as the children of the King is also played out in a powerful parable of the Dubno Maggid:

There was once a righteous king and queen who were loved by all their subjects. Sadly, they were not blessed with children for many years. When at last a daughter was born to them, the entire kingdom celebrated. The princess grew up in the royal palace and learned to live up to her station as the daughter of the king.

When the princess reached marriageable age, the king began to search the land to find a young man who would be fitting to assume the role of prince. After a long search, a fine young man was chosen to become the prince and the wedding date was set. It was a beautiful wedding celebrated with much pomp and fanfare. The young couple looked perfect together as they set out on a life full of promise and potential.

After their wedding, the prince and princess bid a tearful farewell to the king and moved to a faraway palace where they would begin their new life together. At first, the prince was a very good husband who treated his wife with respect and honor. But as time wore on, the prince's new role as a member of the royal household began to fade, and his old life as a commoner began to re-emerge. As it did, he began treating his wife with disrespect. He relegated her to perform menial chores and subjected her to coarse, unrefined treatment.

The princess despaired. Her inbred purity rebelled at the life she was being forced to live, and yet, there was nothing she could do. The princess began to feel like a maidservant.

One day, a letter came from the king announcing that, having been distant from his daughter for almost a year, he would be visiting his daughter and son-in-law. As soon as the prince heard that the king was coming, there was an immediate change in him. He began to treat the princess with respect again, as he prepared for the imminent arrival of the king.

When the day of the king's arrival finally came, the prince dressed in his finest clothing and welcomed him with great honor. The princess saw that the presence of her royal father was bringing out the best in her husband. Overnight, he turned into a fine gentleman once again, and she was delighted to have her royal husband back for as long as it would last.

After two weeks, the king prepared to return to his palace and resume his royal duties. "I am pleased to see that your husband is living up to his position as a prince," he told his daughter. "It is wonderful to see you so happy."

As the princess escorted her father to his royal carriage, she bravely tried to maintain a smiling demeanor, even though she dreaded the moment he would leave her once again at the mercy of her husband. Finally, she could hold back her feelings no longer

"Father! Father! Please don't go!" she cried out. "Don't leave me here alone with this man! It's not the way you think. My husband is not at all how he appears. He mistreats me, but now that you are here, he is putting on a show. As soon as you leave, he will revert back to his evil ways! Father, I need you to stay here with me! I can't bear it any longer!"

The Dubno Maggid explains: Hashem took our holy *neshamah* and searched to match it with a prince, with whom it would live a life of purity and holiness. That prince is the body, whose job is to take good care of the soul, making sure that it is nourished in this world by learning Torah and performing mitzvos. However, as time passes, the body starts to revert back to its natural ways. It forgets the spiritual needs of the princess and indulges in the pleasures of the world, badly mistreating its soulmate. The soul suffers, as it is forced to bear the impure actions of the body.

Finally, the month of Elul arrives. The shofar is blown, heralding the imminent arrival of the king. Suddenly, the body is reminded of its purpose in the world. We therefore begin to pray and perform mitzvos with renewed dedication. The *Yamim Noraim* are the King's two-week visit with his princess. In proximity to the King, the body realizes that it is a member of the royal family, and must act accordingly. But then the princess sees that the King's visit is coming to an end and knows that her prince will soon return to his old ways.

The soul's desperate longing to stay in the presence of her Father, the King, pours out of her at Ne'ilah, when the heavenly gates begin to close and our Father in heaven is set to return to His throne. She cries out, "Father, don't leave me here alone! I can't bear to live without Your Presence!"

The Dubno Maggid's parable ends there. He does not provide us with the response of the King to his daughter's plea. I once heard a beautiful response that would comfort the daughter.

Upon hearing the princess' cries, the king looks into her eyes as tears stream down his face. "My dearest daughter, I can't take you with me because your destiny is here with your prince. That is what is best for you. But I have an idea. Build for me an extension to your home where I will be able to come and be with you each year for seven days.

"During those days, I will spend time living with the prince. We will dine together and spend hours in deep conversation, and he will thus be able to learn from my example how to live up to his role as a member of the royal family."

In this spirit, Hashem our King commands us to build an attachment to our homes, a *succah,* where He can dwell with us each year for seven days. During those days, we spend time with Him, learning how to live in the presence of the King. We see that we, too, can live a life of purity and spirituality for an extended period of time, and thus even when the King finally parts from us, the lesson will last throughout the year. We will no longer be commoners playing the role of princes; we will become true princes.

If we bring Hashem into our lives throughout the year by constantly placing Him before our eyes in our daily actions, acting and speaking with dignity, then in essence, we will be living with the King always. And while the King is with us, He will shower us with many gifts — parnassah, good health, and success.

The Best Defense

In a lecture given in Monsey before Rosh Hashanah, Rabbi Zecharia Wallerstein related the following story. It offers a powerful strategy for success on our day of judgment, so that we may merit a good New Year and a life of blessing.

The story was splashed all over the newspapers and talked about on every radio station. A major figure in politics was accused of murder, and a million-dollar defense attorney had taken his case. An assistant district attorney, a young man who had just graduated law school, was chosen as the prosecutor. Common wisdom said that the young lawyer had no chance to win. The pundits were predicting that the state would come out looking foolish and the defendant would win without even trying.

The prosecutor opened his case by painting a sympathetic picture of the victim, a girl who would never have the chance to get married, have children, and contribute her gifts to the world. He demanded justice for the man who had snuffed out this promising young life.

The defense lawyer then took the floor to present his side of the case. He described his client as a devoted public servant who had often come to the aid of his constituents as well as his family and friends. "He is a good man with a good record, and he is being accused of a crime he did not commit," the attorney stated.

The prosecutor began calling his witnesses to testify. Step by step, he attempted to build his case. The defense lawyer, however, seemed almost disengaged from the proceedings. He did not bother to cross examine the witnesses, nor did he offer any evidence in rebuttal to their testimony. The spectators began wondering what the million-dollar lawyer was doing to earn his fee. Even more baffled was the accused man, who was paying that huge fee and whose life was hanging on the outcome of the trial.

At the end of the trial, each side had its turn to give a summation. The prosecutor rose to his feet and stated that although the body of the girl had not been found, his expert witnesses had proven beyond a doubt that the defendant had murdered her.

"Now I leave it up to you, the jury, to bring this man to justice by finding him guilty and ensuring that law will be upheld," he concluded grandly.

The defense lawyer then rose to offer his summation. Every eye was focused on him, wondering what he would say to explain his bizarre strategy in this case.

"You are all probably wondering why I didn't offer much of a defense for my client," he began. "You probably thought I had lost my touch, but let me ask you all a question. Why would I defend a man whose innocence could easily be proven?

"Let me tell you all something that happened a week ago. I received a phone call from Mexico. Do you know who called me? It was the supposed victim in this case. The girl had simply run away from home and didn't want her parents to find her. That is why there is no body to be found. The girl is alive and well, and when she realized that this man was going to be put to death for her alleged murder, she came to her senses and decided that she would save an innocent man's life. She informed me that she would be arriving in the courthouse today.

"In fact, she called me today during the court's recess and told me she would be here in court at 4 p.m. I have not offered a defense nor a summation today, because at 4 p.m., the case will be solved for good."

A buzz of excitement overtook the courtroom. "They could have killed an innocent man!" one person shouted. "This whole case is a joke!" said another. The court reporters were scribbling furiously and any sense of order evaporated in the drama and confusion. The judge banged his gavel and called for order.

"We will give the defendant until 4 p.m. before sending the jury out for a verdict," the judge announced.

Every person sitting in the courtroom could feel the mounting tension as the clock crept toward 4 p.m. But the moment came and went without event. People glanced at the door every few minutes. Suddenly, at 4:30, the door swung open and the people in the courtroom began rising from their seats to see the alleged victim enter the room. They quickly plopped down again when they recognized the entering woman as one of the court stenographers.

At 5, the judge had had his fill. "I don't know what is going on here," he told the defense lawyer, but your time is up. Either you give your summation now or I will send the jury out without it." The attorney began to speak.

"Ladies and gentleman of the jury, I am sure that you are well aware of the law in America, that in order to find someone guilty, the case must be proven beyond a reasonable doubt. I would now like to ask the members of the jury this question. From 4 o'clock until 5 o'clock, were you all not looking at the door to see if the girl would walk through?

"Now, if you knew beyond a reasonable doubt that the defendant was guilty of killing that girl, why were you looking at the door? You would have known that she could not walk in."

Then he turned to the judge and said, "Your honor, you too had your eyes glued to that door waiting to see if the girl would walk through. You, too, jumped out of your seat when the door opened at 4:30. This means that all of you really believed she was going to walk through that door. Therefore, it is clear that you never believed beyond a reasonable doubt that my client was guilty, and you have no choice but to find the defendant not guilty."

The court was abuzz again, with words like "brilliant" and "perfect defense" surfacing above the din. The judge called for order and instructed the jury to assemble in the jury room and render a verdict.

As the defense lawyer had predicted, they came back in a mere five minutes. The foreman rose to read the verdict. Looking straight at the defendant, he solemnly intoned, "We, the jury, find the defendant guilty of first-degree murder."

Once again, the courtroom erupted into chaos. Loudest among the shouts were those of the defense attorney. "This is a mistrial! How could that be?" he demanded. But the verdict had been rendered and there was nothing left to say. The defendant was led away to await sentencing. But the lawyer couldn't rest. As he exited the courtroom, he approached the foreman.

"What happened?" he asked. "How could you have denied what everyone so clearly saw?"

The foreman called over a woman who had been part of the jury. "She can explain," said the foreman. "She was the one who noticed."

"Noticed what?" the attorney demanded.

"While everyone else was looking at the door, I was looking at the defendant," she explained. "Not once did he glance at the door. Not once did he indicate in any way that he really believed the woman would walk in. Even when the door opened at 4:30, he didn't turn his head. Now, he is the only one who would really know whether she could possibly walk in, and if he didn't show any indication that he believed his own story, then he must have known that she was dead."

Later, visiting his client in jail, the lawyer told him what the juror had said. "You were a fool," he told his client. "Just one glance in the right direction, just one sign that this story might be true, and we would have won the case."

The politician's case is like our own as we stand before Hashem on Rosh Hashanah, says Rabbi Wallerstein. "We stand there and plead for our lives as this million-dollar lawyer was doing. We tell our story — this year is going to be different; we are really going to change and be good. We have the best lawyers, the defending angels who are pleading our case before Hashem. But if we don't turn around and look at the door, if we don't show that we believe our story by acting on the inspiration and making changes in our lives, then we disprove our own case. The *satan* (prosecuting angel) can then argue, "I know he is guilty because he didn't change at all. He didn't believe his own story. If only he would have looked at the door for a moment, he would have won."

Each of us at our own level must look at the door, look into our souls and see what we can do to become better. And although we may not be perfect, and we won't become tzaddikim overnight, we prove our case by doing the best we can.

I recently met a former IDF soldier who told me a story that really amplifies this lesson.

Zevi, a religious soldier in an elite unit, had to undergo very rigorous training to prepare for the special operations he would be called upon to perform. To survive this training, a soldier had to internalize one idea: There's no such thing as "I can't." By putting themselves to the test every day, taking on feats that seemed impossible and then accomplishing them, the soldiers learned that whatever they truly set their minds to doing, they could do.

On this particular day, the impossible feat was a rope climb. This was not just a normal rope climb; rather, the soldiers had to ascend a rough, 20-foot rope using their hands alone. Feet, legs, and body had to hang limp while the hands did the entire job. The rope hung from a bar, and the soldiers had to touch the bar before they lowered themselves back down in the same manner as they had ascended. The last hurdle was at the very end, when they were within reach of the floor. At that point, they had to keep their feet suspended until the commander gave them permission to alight.

When Zevi's turn came, he climbed the rope quickly, touched the top and began to lower himself down. He reached the bottom and, feet dangling, waiting for the order to land. Instead, the commander said "*od paam*" — do it again.

Already exhausted from the first effort, Zevi could not imagine how he would muster the strength to repeat the entire ordeal. However, he knew he had no option but to try. He worked his way back up the rope, but the muscles in his arms were burning and trembling, and his hands began to bleed from the friction. He kept on pushing himself hand over hand when, just a few feet from the top, his strength gave way and he dropped 18 feet to the floor.

Pain shot through his shoulder, on which he had landed with a tremendous thump. As he lay there writhing, wondering if he had dislocated his shoulder or perhaps even broken something, his commander walked over to him and said, "*Zevi, od paam.*"

In Zevi's mind, a silent shout of protest screamed, "I can't do it!" But he could not allow himself to hold onto those words for long. With energy that was more simulated than real, he rose from the floor, strode over to the rope and began again, ignoring the pain and pretending to himself that this time, he might make it to the top. As he got halfway up the rope, he once again let go and came crashing to the ground. This time the commander told him *"tov meod, Zevi"* — very good.

Lying on the floor, bruised and spent, Zevi did not feel defeated. He felt a surge of pride. He had made an attempt to do what he thought was impossible. He found the strength within himself to push the limit, and in doing so, discovered inner resources he didn't know he had.

After he left the army, Zevi applied this concept to life as a Jew, and used his experience to inspire newly observant Jews. "Sometimes a person feels that it is too hard for him to perform mitzvos, to keep Shabbos and kashrus. We might feel that we don't have the inner strength to do it all. But that rope climb taught me that we have to give it our all, and sometimes even after you've given what you think is your all, you have to dig a little deeper into your soul. You will see that you have the inner strength to do whatever you put your mind to doing."

Sometimes it might seem impossible to keep climbing the spiritual ladder that a Jew has to climb, but we do not have the option to say, "We can't do it." And even if we seem to fail, the fact that we gave it our all is the ultimate success.

Like the rope climber, we thrive on challenge. That is why the yetzer hara is always on duty, telling us the task is impossible. Hashem wants us to constantly be in battle mode, so that we can have the incomparable satisfaction of achieving hard-won goals, as Rabbi Yitzchok Grossman, the great kiruv rabbi of Migdal Ohr, teaches us in the following story:

Walking up the steps of a sprawling Florida mansion, I prepared my thoughts. The wealthy man who owned this estate had agreed to meet me, and I hoped to convince him to give a substantial donation to help my organization. Our meeting was arranged for a Sunday morning, and I arrived right on time.

I knocked on the large oak doors, and to my surprise, the gentle impact pushed them open. I peered inside to see if anyone was there to greet me. I didn't see anyone, so I assumed that someone had left the doors open so that I would let myself in. I stepped into a spacious center hall and looked around. In the room in front of me, a man sat in a comfortable leather armchair. His back was toward me, and in front of him was a very large television screen.

So preoccupied was he with the screen that he did not hear me enter, nor did he hear me announce my arrival. I stood there watching him, waiting to catch his attention. On the screen, a boxing match was taking place. I had never seen anything like it before; two hulking men were punching each other with all their might, trying to knock out the other man. My host was so engrossed in the fight that he began to yell to his favorite combatant, "Come on man, hit him harder, knock him out! Kill him!" He jumped out of his seat with excitement and started to dance around and punch in the air as if he himself were in the ring.

Finally, there was a break in the action. Again I said, "Shalom!"

My host whipped his head around and his face registered surprise and embarrassment. He realized that his shouting and play-boxing had been seen by an audience.

"Oh, Rabbi, I'm so sorry," he said quickly. "I didn't realize you were there ... obviously. Please, please come in and have a seat. I really must apologize ..."

"There's no need!" I interrupted. "There's nothing to apologize for. As a matter of fact, you helped me answer a question that has been bothering one of my students for a long time."

"I did?" he asked.

"Yes, you did. You see, one of my students has asked me several times, if Hashem wants us to learn Torah and do mitzvos, why would he create us with a *yetzer hara* that pulls us in the opposite direction. Wouldn't we accomplish more without it?

"And here is how you answered the question. Hashem created us with a *yetzer hara* because the purpose of our being in this world is to face the challenge of the *yetzer hara* and overcome it. Can you imagine watching that boxing match if there were only one fighter in the ring? We are only excited when there's a battle to be won. It's as if Hashem is looking down from heaven, watching the fight unfold. Hashem is rooting for us up there, 'Come on Yankel, knock out your *yetzer hara.* Don't give in to your urges.' Our job is to fight as hard as we can, and win the championship."

With the help of Hashem, we will always emerge as true champions over the yetzer hara.

A Blast From the Past

Hashem loves every Jew like a father loves his son, for even if a son has strayed off the path, his father awaits his eventual return. In the same way, Hashem loves every Jew, and even if he does not observe the Torah and mitzvos, Hashem awaits the day when he will connect to his Father in Heaven. In fact, sometimes Hashem sends a messenger to hasten the process of return.

In the summer of 2011, Rabbi Yaakov Ringler,* the spiritual leader of a community in Israel, traveled to Miami Beach, Florida, to tend to some business. While he was there, he took the opportunity to visit his uncle Morris, whom he had not seen in many years.

Uncle Morris was a Holocaust survivor who had shed his Jewish observances soon after he hit the shores of America. All he wanted was to be a "normal" person living a "normal" life in the American melting pot. He married Becky, a survivor who shared his outlook, and they settled down to a life devoted to building a family and enjoying the freedom and opportunity their adopted home country had to offer. Eventually, they retired and moved to Florida.

Rabbi Ringler had always felt a special affection for his uncle, despite the difference in their lifestyles. Likewise, Uncle Morris felt close to his religious nephew, Yaakov. So when Yaakov called to say that he was in from Israel and wanted to visit, Uncle Morris was elated. "Sure, come right over!" he told his nephew. He and his wife instantly sprang into action preparing cake and coffee to feed their guest.

Weaving through the streets of Uncle Morris' condo community, Rabbi Ringler at last arrived at the right building. The neat carpet of grass punctuated by lush flowering bushes created a paradise-like backdrop for the stucco-and-tile houses. No wonder Uncle Morris was so willing to leave New York behind, thought Rabbi Ringler as he arrived at his uncle's door.

He was lifting his hand to knock when he stopped in midstream. A beautifully carved silver *mezuzah* shone from the doorpost. "That's funny," Rabbi Ringler thought. "I don't think they ever had a *mezuzah* before. Well, maybe it was a gift from someone and they hung it up to be polite."

He finished knocking. Moments later, he and his uncle were embracing tightly, stepping back to get a look at each other, and then embracing some more. "You look younger, not older!" Yaakov Ringler told his uncle. "Florida really agrees with you."

As Uncle Morris led his guest to the dining-room table, there were more surprises on hand. A silver Shabbos *leichter* (candelabra) stood tall in the middle of the table. Along the wall was a large oak bookcase, and lined up on the shelves were a variety of *siddurim, Chumashim,* and other *sefarim.* Rabbi Ringler looked at the "evidence" and then looked at his uncle and aunt, who were by now quite obviously studying their nephew's expression.

"All right," Rabbi Ringler said. "I see that a lot has changed here, Uncle Morris. What happened?"

"Yaakov, sit down and have some cake and let me tell you a story." This is the story Uncle Morris told:

As you know, I haven't been a religious man since the war, and I have not been in a shul in many years. Even on Rosh Hashanah I wouldn't go. Even though there was an Orthodox shul right across the street from me, I could not get myself to set foot there. But that all changed last Rosh Hashanah.

During the afternoon on Rosh Hashanah, I was out on my porch relaxing. I was enjoying my view of the beautiful sea. The sky was perfectly clear and the sand on the beach was sparkling. Suddenly, I noticed a group of Jewish men in their suits and hats walking from the shul toward the water. I wondered why they would be going to the beach when it was such a holy day for them.

I had no idea what they were up to and was very curious to know. I had forgotten that there was such a concept of *tashlich,* and these men were headed toward the water to throw their sins into the sea. My curiosity got me out of my beach chair and I began to walk toward the group to find out what was going on. In a way, it was my little baby step toward observing the Yom Tov. If I wasn't going to go to shul to be with other Jews on this holy day, then at least I could join them at the beach.

When I reached the group, I saw that they were all holding *siddurim* in their hands and they were saying a prayer. I still didn't understand why they had to come out here instead of praying in their nice air-conditioned shul. One of the men noticed me standing there and came over to me with a *siddur* in his hand. He pointed to the place and told me to say a prayer.

As I stood there, my memory was jogged and I recalled going

out to the water with my father when I was a little boy back in our town in Poland. I recalled that the idea was to take our sins and throw them into the sea. I became all emotional as memories of my youth began to flood my mind. I began to cry, and I started to pour out my heart to Hashem for the first time in my adult life. As I was crying, thinking about my childhood and how I prayed with my father in the town's big shul, I suddenly felt a tap on my back.

"Excuse me, would you like to hear the shofar today?" said the voice behind me in a rich Yiddish, the likes of which I had not heard in many years.

I turned around and saw standing behind me an old man with a short white beard whose face appeared to shine. I was impressed by his aristocratic appearance and I immediately answered that I had not yet heard shofar-blowing today, and would appreciate if he would blow the shofar for me.

The old man put his hand into his pocket and pulled out a very tiny shofar. It looked very old. He began to blow the sweetest sounds from that shofar — sounds that went straight into my heart. I was really moved by the *tashlich* and especially by the beautiful sound of the shofar, and I wondered, who was this man who had sought me out? I didn't recognize him from the neighborhood. In fact, he seemed to really stand out in the crowd.

When he finished blowing the shofar, he turned to me and spoke again in his rich Yiddish "I hope you enjoyed the shofar blowing. My name is Moshe Katz. Good luck!" He then turned around and left.

I came home a few minutes later and related the whole story to Aunt Becky. I told her about *tashlich*, and then I told her about my strange encounter with this man who blew shofar for me. I described how the man looked and how he had been carrying this tiny shofar with such a beautiful sound. Aunt Becky asked me the man's name. When I answered "Moshe Katz," her face suddenly turned pale and she collapsed to the floor.

I ran to her side and brought her back to consciousness. The moment she opened her eyes, she asked me to tell her the name again. So I did.

"I can't believe it!" she cried out.

"Believe what?" I asked her. "Do you know this person?"

"That wasn't just a person," she said. "That was my father!"

"Katz? But your family name is Coles. And your father is gone, just like the rest of the family. The Nazis took your father 60 years ago."

"Katz was my family name," Aunt Becky explained. "I changed it to Coles when I came here so that I would blend in better. My father was the *baal tokei'a* (shofar blower) in our shul, and he had a tiny shofar, just like the one you described.

"Becky, take a deep breath," I told her. "You're imagining things."

She got up from the floor and ran to our bedroom. A few minutes later, she came out holding an old photo album. She pointed out a picture to me — a picture that had been somehow preserved from the old country. And do you know what it was, Yaakov? It was her father — the man I saw on the beach. And he was holding a little shofar to his lips — the exact shofar he blew for me.

Yaakov, it became so clear. Hashem had sent Aunt Becky's holy father here to give us a message. It's time to do *teshuvah*. Time is wasting and we won't live forever. Hashem waited and waited for us, and when we didn't come back to Him, He sent us this message. It was undeniable, even for two non-believers like Aunt Becky and me.

Well, that was it. From that day on, we have been keeping Shabbos and kashrus, and we are learning more and growing every day. I bought myself a pair of *tefillin* and started going to shul. I am returning to Hashem because He wants me. There can be no other explanation. That is why everything has changed here.

When Morris took his first step back toward Hashem — a step out onto the beach to join the Jews performing tashlich — Hashem performed a miracle to carry him the rest of the way home. When we open our hearts just a bit to let a little of Hashem's light enter, He responds by illuminating our entire soul.

Fight for Me

Hashem constantly sends us messages to let us know that He is watching over us and waiting for us to return to Him. Sometimes, perceiving these messages takes close scrutiny and deep thinking. Sometimes, however, the message is as clear as day.

Dozens of women crowded into the modest home of Rebbetzin Batsheva Kanievsky. Under this humble roof on Rechov Rashbam in Bnei Brak, the hopes, fears, doubts, and dreams of women from across the spectrum of Jewish life found a listening ear and a loving, accepting heart. And on this day, 20-year-old Reva and her mother were among these women. They would have to wait their turn, but Reva's mother silently, desperately prayed that the wait would prove worthwhile.

It had already been years since Reva had parted ways with her pious family. She made it clear that she wanted no part of their lifestyle. She dressed, ate, socialized, and lived as she wished. Her mother kept hoping and praying, telling herself that the situation could always turn around. *Teshuvah* could happen in an instant. But if Reva were to take the next step, the fateful step she was planning to take, she could never turn it around. Her life would be changed forever.

Out of the corner of her eye, Reva's mother studied her daughter. Her heart ached as she remembered naming her in shul. "She will be called in Israel ..." What hopes her parents had for the child bearing that name! They sent her off to Bais Yaakov with dreams of leading her to her *chuppah*. Now, Reva was employed in a local store, and one of her fellow employees, an Arab man, had charmed her into believing that they could marry and live happily ever after.

"You can't make a decision like this without speaking to someone," Reva's mother had urged her.

"I'm not speaking to anyone," Reva had replied adamantly. "I'm done speaking. No one will understand my point of view, anyway. There is no point in talking about it."

Reva's mother made one last effort. "How about speaking to Rebbetzin Kanievsky?" she suggested. "All kinds of women go to her. She accepts everyone. She understands everyone. She'll listen to what you have to say."

Reva knew well that the Rebbetzin was a source of succor and guidance for Jews from all over the world. She knew of the legendary warmth and love that flowed from this holy woman Why not, at this important juncture in life, experience a meeting with Rebbetzin Kanievsky?

And so, the mother and daughter sat waiting their turn. At last, Reva was ushered into the simple, age-worn room where souls were healed.

As the conversation progressed, Reva began to feel that there was nothing new to discover here. The Rebbetzin, in her motherly way, was trying to impress the young woman with the grandeur of being a Bas Yisrael. But Reva wasn't looking for grandeur. The words rolled off her like rain off a rooftop. The Rebbetzin perceived that reason would not work — she could throw Reva life-line after life-line of beautiful concepts and irrefutable reasons, but Reva wouldn't grab the line.

The Rebbetzin stopped speaking for a moment. A new approach was needed. She looked Reva in the eye and spoke directly, yet kindly.

"Listen to me, my dear. I want you to take at least upon yourself one thing for Hashem. This one thing will keep your connection alive and bring you great *berachah*."

"What is it that you would like me to do?" asked Reva.

"I want you to say one chapter of *Tehillim* each day."

"All right, that is something that I would be willing to do."

The Rebbetzin walked over to the table and picked up a small *Tehillim* and handed it to Reva. "Let's start right away. We'll say it together."

The Rebbetzin opened the *Tehillim* to a random page, which happened to be Chapter 43, and began to read the first verse: "*Shofteni Elokim ve'****riva rivi migoy lo chasid*** *me'ish mirmah v'avlah sefalteini* — Avenge me, O G-d, and fight my cause against a nation unkind; rescue me from a man of deceit and iniquity."

As the young woman began to repeat the words after the Rebbetzin, she suddenly choked up and could not finish the sentence. She felt the prickle of tears filling her eyes; she could not force the emotion back down into the depths from which it had erupted. The tears turned to torrents; the prayer turned to sobbing.

"I can't marry him!" she declared.

The Rebbetzin waited for the young woman to work through the emotions that had beset her. She wondered with amazement at the power of those few words of *Tehillim* to ignite immediate *teshuvah* in a heart that seemed so far away.

At last, Reva composed herself. "My name is Reva," she said. "I see that Hashem is calling to me through the *Tehillim: Riva rivi migoy* — *Reva!* Fight for My cause, and don't marry this goy ... *Me'ish mirmah v'avlah sefalteini* — Rescue yourself from this man of deceit and iniquity.

"Rebbetzin, how else can anyone explain why the *Tehillim* opened to the exact verse that hints to my name? I see Hashem wants me to return."

Reva promised the Rebbetzin that she would not marry the Arab man, and would try her best to do sincere *teshuvah*. Rather than fighting her family and her heritage, she would do what Hashem had directly requested of her: "Fight for My cause."

Sometimes when problems come our way, we think, "It's a message from Hashem, but WHAT IS the message? What does He want me to do?" Yet, when we open our hearts, we know what we have to do, and we realize what Hashem has been trying to tell us all along.

A Belated Bar Mitzvah

Deep down within himself, every Jew feels a connection with his Creator. However, sometimes those feelings are buried beneath layers of pain or anger. Nevertheless, Hashem always waits for His children to come back, even if it takes many years.

Simcha Kranzer* was a young man who had a mission. True to his name, he loved to bring other people happiness. That was what motivated him to begin visiting the local Jewish nursing home on a regular basis. There he found many elderly Jews who, with just a smile and a few friendly words, could be brought from boredom and loneliness back to life.

Eventually, though, the quick smile and hello didn't seem to be enough. He wanted to do something that would really improve their quality of life, all day every day. Something that would lift their spirits and give them a reason to want to wake up in the morning. "A Shacharis *minyan*!" he decided. "That's what they need here."

To get his *minyan* started, he showed up one day at breakfast time and announced that there would be a Shacharis every morning in the nursing home's shul. He canvassed the potential attendees to see whom he could expect, and found out that while many would like to come, they had difficulty getting there on their own. Simcha found a solution: he would come 20 minutes early and gather up whoever could not get to the shul by himself.

Every morning, Simcha arrived and took his list of Jewish residents in hand. He popped his friendly face into each room and inquired if they would like to join the *minyan*. After only a few days, his appearance became an eagerly awaited feature of the morning routine. The men loved the *minyan* so much that they even stayed for a while after it to learn together.

Only one man had a sour reaction to Simcha's morning visits. That was Mr. Newman.* Whenever Simcha showed up, he would turn to him and scowl, "Leave me alone, young man. I told you I'm not interested in a *minyan*."

Simcha thought that perhaps he should leave Mr. Newman alone as he demanded, but something told him that it was still worth an effort. If only he could break through to the man, he was sure that he could bring him something that would add happiness and meaning to his last years. With that in mind, he was willing to pay the price of a brief daily encounter with what appeared to be a stubborn old man.

One morning, Simcha decided to try a new approach to Mr. Newman. As usual, he stuck his head in the door and invited the elderly man to Shacharis. And as usual, Mr. Newman rebuffed him rudely. Instead of leaving, though, Simcha turned to him with a soft smile and said, "Mr. Newman, please don't scream at me anymore ... I don't mean to bother you. I truly feel that you would enjoy the *minyan* if you would just give it a chance. Why are you so against it?"

Mr. Newman's hard demeanor instantly fell away. "Have a seat, young man," he told Simcha. "Let me explain a few things to you.

You see, you think I don't want to go to the *minyan,* but the fact is, I cannot go."

"Sure you can, Mr. Newman. I'll take you. It's no trouble!"

"No, no, no. It has nothing to do with getting there," he said sadly. "Let me tell you a story and you will understand."

I am a Holocaust survivor. I was a young boy of 12 when the Nazis took me and my father away. We were brought to a concentration camp where we were forced to do backbreaking labor. My father did his best to keep my spirits up, but it was so difficult for me to be taken away from my mother and my home at such a tender age. Somehow, though, we managed to make a routine. My father and I shared our meals together and he would always teach me to believe that Hashem would take us out of that nightmare alive.

One day, my father came over to me and said, "Son, you are 12 years old now, but tomorrow is your birthday and you will be a bar mitzvah *bachur*. Although we won't be able to have a bar mitzvah celebration as we would have loved to have, I would like you to have the opportunity to put on *tefillin*. I have done some research and have discovered that there are two people in camp who have managed to smuggle in *tefillin*.

On our side of the camp, there is a man who has a *tefillin shel rosh* (*tefillin* for the head) but on the other side of the camp, I heard that there is a man who has a complete set, a *tefillin shel rosh* and *a tefillin shel yad (tefillin* for the hand*)*. In honor of your bar mitzvah, I want you to put on a complete pair. So I plan to sneak to the other side of camp before dawn and bring you a complete pair to put on.

"No, father, please don't go. It's too dangerous," I told him. "If they catch you, you know they'll kill you on the spot and I'll be left all alone. I am willing to forgo putting on *tefillin* to have you here with me."

But my father wouldn't be dissuaded. He only wanted to do what a father should do for his son, even if everything around us conspired against it. He told me that he would be extra careful and would not get caught. I saw that it was no use arguing.

In middle of the night, my father silently left the barracks and crept to the other side of the camp while I watched in fear. The time moved so slowly. I was sure the worst had happened. But just as I began to fall into despair, I caught sight of him from afar, keeping to the corners and shadows of the camp as he carried the *tefillin* toward our barracks. My excitement was mounting as he got closer and closer. In just a few minutes, he would be safe by my side.

Suddenly, a sharp yell pierced the quiet night. It was the unmistakable sound of a German command to halt. My heart pounded in my ears as I watched a horrible scene unfold in front of my eyes. The Nazi raised his gun, the sound of the shot echoed through the camp and my father crumpled to the ground. The *tefillin* dropped alongside him.

I waited until the Nazi had gone and ran out to see if perhaps my father had only been wounded. But the German's aim had been precise. My father was no more. I grabbed the *tefillin* and ran back to my barracks, my heart torn by a grief that knew no bounds. And that is how my bar mitzvah day began.

Mr. Newman finished his story and looked into my eyes. "Do you see why I can't go to shul? How can I ever come to terms with what happened? How can I ever pray to a G-d Who let my father be killed as he tried to bring me *tefillin*?"

"That is such a sad story, Mr. Newman," I sympathized. As I looked at him now, I saw the bereft orphan that he was 60 years ago, and remained throughout his life. But I knew that carrying around this burden of grief had not given him peace. "Let me ask you this, though. Don't you think that your father would have wanted you to put on your *tefillin*?"

"Maybe, but it brings back such painful memories," he said. "But in honor of my father, I still keep them around." He reached over to his night table and extracted an old worn-out bag of *tefillin* from the drawer. "See, here it is. It reminds me of my father, but putting them on is a whole different story."

Simcha accepted Mr. Newman's words and left the room, but in his heart, he resolved that he would get Mr. Newman to put on those *tefillin* one day soon.

The opportunity arose just a few days later. Simcha had gathered the men for Shacharis, but one of the regulars was sick and another didn't show up. He was left with only nine men. Simcha told everyone that he would try to get Mr. Newman to come and be the tenth man. No one believed that he would succeed, but Simcha was going to try.

Simcha came into Mr. Newman's room and told him, "I've got a problem, Mr. Newman. Maybe you can help me. You see, I've been successful in putting a *minyan* together every day for the past month. The men really enjoy it and I would hate to have to cancel it, but today, we are missing a tenth man. I was wondering if I could just bring you over there to be the tenth. You won't have to do anything."

Not wanting to deprive his fellow residents of something they found uplifting, Mr. Newman agreed to be present. "You make sure to keep my wheelchair in the back of the room so that I can be the first one to leave, and I will just sit there," he said. "I am not going to pray with you guys."

Simcha agreed to his conditions. As Simcha was wheeling him out of the room, he asked, "Mr. Newman, can we bring along your *tefillin*?"

"We can bring them along," he said. "It's a good place for them to be. But I'm not wearing them."

They retrieved the *tefillin* from the night table and Simcha brought Mr. Newman to the shul. With his arrival, the *minyan* had its tenth man and began davening. Simcha handed Mr. Newman a *tallis*, which he wrapped around himself. Someone else handed him a *siddur.* Meanwhile, the rest of the men were donning their *tefillin.*

Mr. Newman signaled to Simcha to come over to him. "Can you help me out a little? I think I'll try to put these on after all," he said, holding out his *tefillin* bag.

It was the moment Simcha had been waiting for. He gently removed the *tefillin* from the worn velvet bag and assisted Mr. Newman in wrapping them around his hand and head. As he worked to properly wrap and secure the straps, he saw two rivers of tears coursing down the old man's face. Simcha finished the job and stood back. Mr. Newman pulled the *tallis* over his head and began to daven for the first time in decades.

He remembered some of the *tefillos* from his youth, and as he said them, he touched the deep, pure part of his heart that had been buried so long ago. The faithful and pure 12-year-old who trusted Hashem and loved Him was at last reawakened.

That day was a Monday, so the *minyan* would be reading from the Torah. Simcha knew exactly whom he would call up for an *aliyah*. He found out that Mr. Newman was a Levi and called him up for the Levi *aliyah*. Mr. Newman appeared shocked by the honor; a man who had not set foot in shul in 60 years, suddenly asked to make the blessing on the Torah? He was wheeled to the table that held the Torah scroll and Simcha guided him through the words of the *berachah*. His voice broken with emotion, he struggled to speak loudly enough to be heard by the other men.

Davening concluded, but Mr. Newman was not yet ready to leave. Simcha approached him and asked if he was all right.

"Yes, everything is all right," he said. "You know, you gave me something today that I never had before."

"What is that, Mr. Newman?"

"You gave me a real bar mitzvah," he smiled wistfully. "It might be 60 years late, but you know what? Better late then never. I'll tell you something else, too. You really made someone proud."

By now, Simcha's eyes were welling with tears. "I did? Who, Mr. Newman?"

"I think we made my father proud today. And if there was anything I ever really wanted to do in my life, it was to make my father proud of his little boy." With those words, Mr. Newman broke down, crying the healing tears he had so long denied himself.

For the rest of that year, Mr. Newman attended the *minyan* daily. He became a big fan of Simcha, who derived the deepest satisfaction from watching his elderly friend proudly don his *tefillin – shel yad* and *shel rosh* – each and every day.

One morning, Mr. Newman was late for Shacharis and Simcha came to his room to find him. That was when he discovered that Mr. Newman had not been feeling well during the night, and had been taken to the hospital, where he passed away. The *levayah* would take place that day.

During the days of *shivah*, Simcha went to pay a condolence call to Mr. Newman's only daughter, a woman who had herself recently become religious. His daughter lit up when she saw Simcha. "You changed my father's life," she told him. "Ever since I could remember, my father had a certain bitterness in his heart toward G-d, but during the last year since he began to put on his *tefillin,* everything changed. He seemed to make peace with his Creator and it's all because of you. My father did real *teshuvah* and lived his last days with true *simchah.*"

No matter what life brings, there is never any joy or peace in cutting ourselves off from Hashem, Who is, after all, the only true Source of our comfort.

Chapter 3:

Loving Hashem With All Your Heart

My Bulletproof Vest

Rabbi Zecharia Wallerstein is the founder and director of Obr Naava, an organization dedicated to inspiring women of all ages. Through his weekly lectures and the various programs that he has developed, Rabbi Wallerstein's impact on the world of chinuch reaches far beyond the classroom, into communities around the world. The story that follows was told over at a shiur and is Rabbi Wallerstein's own story, in which he relates the circumstances that led him to dedicate his life to chinuch. It is a story with a message for everyone.

It's been more than 30 years since I began my career in *chinuch,* but I can still remember clearly the series of events, the thoughts and emotions that led me in this direction.

When I was 9 years old, in third grade, an incident happened that changed my life forever. The yeshivah that I attended had a big yard, and behind that yard was a deep forest. During recess, my friend and I wandered into the forest to play. In our childish minds, we had no idea that what we were doing was dangerous. We just set out to have fun.

Because we were very preoccupied with our fun, and too far away to hear the call to return to class, we remained in the woods after all the other kids had gone in. Our rebbi quickly realized we were missing and reported this fact to the principal immediately. A search party was launched, and soon we heard rebbeim heading toward us in the woods, calling our names in a loud, urgent tone. We quickly surmised that we were in trouble, and so we did what seemed to us to be the logical thing — we walked deeper and deeper into the woods.

When the rebbeim failed to find us, they wasted no time calling in the state troopers, who entered the woods with search dogs. Now we heard not only our names being called, but the fierce barking of the dogs. We tried to run further out of harm's way, but finally, at 4 p.m., after four hours of searching, we were found.

Now our real troubles began. Our principal's fear for our fate had turned into fuming anger, and he was determined to make an example out of us to ensure that no one ever attempted this stunt again. In those days, the norms of *chinuch* were different from the way they are today. Children and parents alike accepted the fact that a rebbi might correct misbehavior with a slap. My friend and I had no doubt that this would be our fate.

Our principal took us into the first-grade class and stood us in front of the class. He stood near me as he announced to the class, "This, boys, is what happens to a boy who runs away from yeshivah." The principal lifted his hand and smacked me on the right side of my face, and then he smacked me again on the left side of my face. I burst into tears from the crushing blow, but accepted it, knowing that I deserved it.

But the principal wasn't done yet. He then brought me into the second grade and announced to the boys, "This is what happens to boys who run away from yeshivah," and he smacked me twice again. Then he brought me to the third, fourth, fifth, sixth, seventh, and finally the eighth grade and slapped me twice in each class. I got smacked a total of 16 times that day.

As the principal was taking me back to the office, where I was going to be suspended, I asked him in innocence, in a tear-choked voice, "Why couldn't you call an assembly for the whole school and just slap me twice?"

"A *mechutzaf* (a disrespectful person)!" he yelled, and he slapped me again. This happened in third grade. Many years have passed since then, and I have long forgotten the physical pain, but I will never ever forget the embarrassment I felt while I stood there receiving those slaps in public.

By the time I got to high school, I was really struggling. If this was what *Yiddishkeit* was about — a 9-year-old getting beaten and embarrassed for running away from school — then maybe I didn't want to be a part of it. I was seriously contemplating jumping out, but there was one thing stopping me. It was my father. He loved his children and gave us the thing that is hardest to give to another person. It's not love, it's time. All a child wants from his parents is their time, and that is what my Dad gave us. It meant more to us than anything in the world.

My Dad was a traveling salesman. He would often leave home on Sunday, drive three days to Florida and drive three days back to New York. On Fridays, I would get home from school at about 2 p.m. and standing there on the porch waiting for me and my brother was my father with a football in his hand. The man had just driven for six days and the first thing he did when he got back home was to play ball and spend some time with his kids.

He always told us, "You need to know one thing, I davened a long time to have you. You are the greatest thing that ever happened to me in my life." As early as I can remember, I knew that was true, not because he said it, but because he showed it. He gave me something that was his, and that was his time.

That is why when a parent gives his children time, they know they are truly loved. It works in *chinuch* too. If a rebbi gives his student time, that means he really cares about that student.

Therefore, as a teenager trying to decide whether or not I would jump out of *Yiddishkeit*, I had one major obstacle. How could I hurt the man who constantly told me that I was the greatest thing in his world? I couldn't do it to him, but I had to do something. I was in the eleventh grade when I made a big life decision: I was not jumping out, I was jumping in.

I decided that I would go into *chinuch* and would be the greatest rebbi in the world. Not one child would ever be embarrassed by me, because I knew what it felt like to be humiliated in front of classmates. I promised myself that I would always protect every child under my auspices. I was 16 at the time, and I had a lot going on in my life. I played basketball and hockey, I played the drums, but I knew one thing for certain — I was going into *chinuch*. And that is why I am where I am today.

My father saved my life because he let me know that I was the greatest thing that ever happened to him. It's not your friends, it's not your business or your money; the most precious thing Hashem ever gave you is your child.

But there is another father that we all have, and that is our Father in Heaven. Every day Hashem says to Bnei Yisrael, "You are the greatest thing in the world to Me. You are My precious children." How can we think of disappointing our Father in Heaven? His love is our bullet-proof vest. Our Father will protect and guide us no matter what, and we in turn will always do our best to make Him proud.

A child who knows he is cherished by his parents has a "bullet-proof vest," a strong protective layer that repels the spiritual dangers that bombard him. Likewise, when each of us internalizes the knowledge that we are cherished children of Hashem, we surround ourselves with the strength to make the right decisions when we are faced with life's challenges

A Woman of Valor

Loving Torah means being willing to go to great lengths for the Torah's sake. It means acting with an understanding that every moment of Torah study is a priceless diamond, the pursuit of which is worthy of every effort. In this story, we learn just how far one woman was willing to go to ensure that not one moment of her husband's learning would be lost.

The partnership between Rebbetzin Shaina Elyashiv and her revered husband, the great *posek hador,* Rav Yosef Shalom Elyashiv, was already in full bloom decades before the Rav became a name renowned throughout the Torah world. The Rebbetzin's entire being was devoted to her husband's learning, and her every action was calculated to ensure that not one moment of it would be lost.

A story told by her daughter, Rebbetzin Batsheva Kanievsky, illustrates the Rebbetzin's loving devotion. Each day, the Rav would awaken at 3 a.m. to begin the rigorous learning schedule to which he adhered. But he would not wake up alone, for his Rebbetzin would rise at that hour as well in order to make him a cup of hot tea.

Knowing of her mother's grueling ritual, Rebbetzin Kanievsky bought her a present. It was a thermos bottle. "With this, you can prepare the tea at night and it will still be piping hot in the morning!" she informed her mother.

Rebbetzin Elyashiv appreciated the gift and the daughterly concern that motivated it. Nevertheless, she turned it down. "There is nothing in the world that I enjoy more than the opportunity to participate in the learning of a *talmid chacham* like your father. I get such a feeling of connection to Hashem by doing this. It wouldn't be the same if I prepared a thermos the night before. Besides, it encourages him to see me push myself to get up early in the morning to help him. He sees that he has a partner in his learning."

This was her way of life throughout the decades, and it did not even desist when she was bedridden with her final illness. As her health began to fail, one of her grandsons moved into the Elyashiv home to assist her, thus leaving the Rav free to learn and to tend to the hundreds of *shailos* that came to him from around the world. The grandson would stay by the Rebbetzin's side throughout the day, and retire to his own room at night.

One night, as the grandson lay in bed trying to fall asleep, he heard a groaning sound coming from somewhere in the house. He wondered in alarm, could it be the Rebbetzin? He hurriedly rose from his bed and ran to his grandparents' room. Peeking into the doorway, he saw that the Rav lay fast asleep, but he was startled to discover that the Rebbetzin's bed was empty. It seemed impossible! How could the Rebbetzin have moved from her bed in her state of weakness?

The grandson felt panic rising up inside him. What could have happened? He ran out to the porch — the direction from which he had heard the groan. There, to his shock, he found his grandmother sitting on the floor, struggling to catch her breath.

"Bubby, are you all right? What are you doing here? How did you get here?" the grandson exclaimed in confusion.

The Rebbetzin's voice was labored. "You know that the *Zeide* doesn't get much sleep at night," she explained. "I woke up with a terrible cough. I was afraid I might wake him up and he wouldn't be able to learn as well if he didn't get enough sleep. I managed to find my way out of my bed and got myself out here to the porch so my coughing wouldn't wake him."

To us, the Rebbetzin's actions seem heroic. To her, however, they were the natural outgrowth of a reverence for Torah that knew no bounds. Even at our own individual levels, however, her example can guide us when we must make our own choices between serving our own needs and serving Hashem.

The Power of Forgiveness

The following story was related by Rabbi Shloime Levenstein, a well-known maggid from Eretz Yisrael. In it, we learn of the pow-

er unleashed in heaven when a person forgives someone who has wronged him.

Sometimes, even a quiet life is turned upside down. That is what happened to Reb Yitzchok,* a *talmid chacham* who lived in Bnei Brak. He earned his *parnassah* as a *cheder* rebbi, and garnered all the excitement he could ever need by watching his students grow in their love of Torah.

His beloved routine was becoming difficult to maintain, however, because he seemed to be suffering from some health issue. He felt tired and physically weak; standing up in class, walking around from student to student, putting life and humor into the day's lessons were becoming a real challenge. Finally, he had to admit that something was wrong. This was no "bug" that would work its way out of his system.

He took himself to the doctor, who recommended some tests. Still, Reb Yitzchok was not worried; it was probably nothing, he reasoned. Why would any dramatic illness sweep into his quiet, orderly life? When the doctor finished reviewing the results of the tests, however, Yitzchok's reasoning exploded in the face of a devastating reality. He was very sick — incurably sick. His remaining life span could be measured in months.

All of his life, Yitzchok had spoken to his students about trust in Hashem. Now he had to prove to himself that he believed his own words. How would he handle this overwhelming news? Would he fall into despair, or turn the situation over to the only One Who could help him? He decided that he would travel to Meiron, to the burial place of Rabbi Shimon bar Yochai, and pour out his heart as he had at other troubling times in his life. He would cry out King David's words of courage and solace, reciting the entire *Sefer Tehillim* as a *zechus* for the Divine assistance he so desperately needed.

These were his thoughts as he left the hospital and walked toward his car, immersed in conversation with himself and his Maker.

He nearly bumped directly into an old acquaintance who had spotted him in the parking lot and was coming over to greet him. As the friend came near, he noticed Yitzchok's pale, sickly complexion.

After a few moments of small talk, the friend could not restrain himself from inquiring into Yitzchok's well-being. "Is everything all right with you?" he asked with sincere concern. "You look so tired."

Not one to burden others with his personal problems, Yitzchok's first instinct was to gloss over his dire situation. But here was a friend, showing up in the right place at the right time, when Yitzchok most needed a listening ear. Yitzchok opened up his heart and laid out all his concerns and fears. "I'm leaving to Meiron to daven at the *kever* of Rabbi Shimon bar Yochai as soon as I can," he told his friend. "It's helped me before, so I'm hoping it will help me now."

"Wait," his friend said. "Before you go, I have one other idea. I work for Kupat Ha-ir (a large charitable organization in Israel) and I work very closely with Rav Chaim Kanievsky. I've seen incredible miracles happen as a result of his *berachos*. Let me bring you to him so that you will get a *berachah* there before you travel to Meiron."

Yitzchok agreed instantly. Soon, the two men were in Rav Chaim's home, telling him about Yitzchok's dire situation. The Rav shook his head gravely.

"It is a very serious situation," he said. "But let me ask you something. Do you remember that I came to visit you in your home eight years ago?"

"Yes, I do," said Yitzchok. It was a visit he could never forget. The representative from Kupat Ha-ir looked at Yitzchok in confusion. "The Rav came to see you in your home?" he asked his friend incredulously.

"Yes, he did," Yitzchok replied.

"Why did he come?" the friend asked.

At this point, Rav Chaim instructed Yitzchok to tell the story, and this is what he said:

Before my wife and I got married, she was engaged to someone and there was a very bitter breakup shortly before the wedding.

She was terribly hurt by the other party and they had left off on very bad terms. But a few months later, my wife met me and we got married, *baruch Hashem.*

We had been married for a few years. We had two children and life was going well. One night, there was a knock on our door. Standing there was Rav Chaim. We were shocked to see that Rav Chaim had come to our house. We had no idea why he had come.

Rav Chaim explained that the family of the boy my wife had been engaged to had been beset by many troubles. Furthermore, the boy himself had married and after several years, was still childless. The Rav explained that all the *berachos* he gave the boy and his family were blocked because of the pain the boy had inflicted on his would-be *kallah*. Therefore, he had come to ask that my wife give them a *ksav mechilah* (a letter of forgiveness).

My wife refused. They had tried to ruin her name with lies and gossip, and this she could not forgive. But Rav Chaim explained that signing the paper would not only bring the boy and his family *berachah* but it would also bring great *berachah* into our home. The Rav stayed in our house speaking to my wife and waiting patiently until finally, she signed the letter with a whole heart.

Rav Chaim took the paper that she signed, handed it to me and said, "Put this in a very safe place."

When Yitzchok reached the end of the story, Rav Chaim asked him, "Do you still have that paper?"

Indeed, Yitzchok had put it away with his valuable documents. He knew just where it was. Rav Chaim instructed him to take the paper with him to Meiron.

"When you are there davening, lift up the paper and show it to Hashem. Tell Him that your wife forgave another Jew who had wronged her and because of this, the man was able to go forward and build a family. Ask that, in that merit, Hashem should keep you healthy so that now your wife can build a family with you."

Yitzchok did as Rav Chaim instructed. He traveled to Meiron with the "evidence" he would bring before the Judge, and begged for his wife's forgiveness to be rewarded by the saving of her husband's life. With all of his heart, with free-flowing tears and passionate words, he prayed for this merit to tip the balance.

A few days after he returned from Meiron, Yitzchok noticed that he was feeling much better. Perhaps unburdening himself in prayer had given him serenity and strength. Or, perhaps ... He returned to the hospital and asked for a new set of tests. The doctors examined him from head to toe and found absolutely no sign of disease. As quickly as his ailment had attacked, it had retreated.

Rabbi Levenstein added this thought: Imagine if eight years earlier, someone would have informed Yitzchok's wife that one day, her husband would be deathly ill and the only way he would be cured would be for her to forgive the person who had hurt her. She surely would have signed the letter immediately. Our trust in Hashem requires us to believe that even when the repercussions are not in clear view, forgiveness will bring a world of blessings our way and protect us in times of danger.

Then Rabbi Levenstein related one more story about the life-altering power of forgiveness:

When Sarah and Rochel, two sisters, converted to Judaism, they imagined that soon they would be married and building families of their own. But the years were moving forward, and the two sisters remained single, living together in their small apartment in Bnei Brak. Although they fully embraced their new lives as Jews, they found Shabbos to be a difficult time. Each week, they would have to look for families to host them so that they could enjoy the full flavor of *zemiros, divrei Torah,* and the company of a warm Jewish family.

One Shabbos, a family they knew from the neighborhood invited them for Shabbos for the first time. The meal started off wonderfully, with the father and children singing *Shalom Aleichem* at a table sparkling with china and glass. They enjoyed the first few courses with the family, and then the main course was served. It was then that the host posed an uncomfortable question.

"It is so amazing that you girls converted to Judaism," he said. "I'm sure it must have been very hard for you. Perhaps you can share with us what it was like to live life as a non-Jew."

The girls were very embarrassed by the question. No one had ever asked it, and they did not feel comfortable discussing their past at the Shabbos table.

"We'd really rather not talk about that," Sarah said politely.

"Why not?" the father asked. "We want to hear the story."

"Well, perhaps some other time then," Sarah responded. "You don't really want to hear about it at the Shabbos table, I'm sure."

"Yes I do!" said the father with mounting irritation. "You're sitting here at our table eating our food, and I think that the least you can do is to give something back by fulfilling one simple request."

The girls' eyes burned with tears of embarrassment that they struggled to hold in check. They glanced at each other and in unison, rose to leave. As they headed to the door, the wife ran after them.

"Please," she said. "Don't leave. You haven't even eaten the meal yet."

"Let them go," the father shouted from his place.

Both girls walked out of the house in tears. They headed down the stairs of the apartment building in which the family lived, eager to get back to the safety of their own little home. Halfway down the stairs, Rochel stopped her sister. "We didn't *bentch*," she said.

"All right," Sarah responded. "We'll stay in the hallway and *bentch* by heart. They began reciting the Blessing After Meals, and arrived at a verse that blesses the host and hostess. They stopped short. "Can we truthfully say this?" Rochel asked her sister. "After what we've just been through, I don't know if we're even allowed to say this."

Sarah took a deep breath. "It's over. They invited us. They prepared for us. Let's just forget the rest." Her sister agreed, and they resumed their *bentching*, offering blessings to the family that hosted them and continuing on to the end.

A few days later, the sisters went to visit Rebbetzin Kanievsky, to whom they often turned for advice. They told her the strange story of their Shabbos experience, and recounted their confusion when they reached the verse of *bentching* that blesses the host. "In the end, we decided to focus on the fact that they were thoughtful enough to invite us and prepare for us, and we overlooked the rest," Rochel reported.

"Do you know what a great thing you did?" the Rebbetzin asked. She seemed sincerely awed by what the girls did. "When a person does not answer back to someone who has insulted him, that person has great power. Girls, you can ask Hashem for anything and in the merit of what you did, you will be answered!"

Sarah and Rochel knew what they wanted. More than anything, they desired homes of their own, husbands of their own, and a Shabbos table of their own. Within the year, both girls got married, and today they each have built a home of *berachah* where everyone is welcome and no one is ever shamed.

There is one final story on this topic that I heard recently and would like to share with you.

The first day of high school was close at hand, and Devora was very nervous. Like all the other girls starting ninth grade, she worried about keeping up with work and making new friends. Unlike the other girls, however, she had a serious reason to worry. Devora's face was terribly disfigured as the result of a fire. She had come to Brooklyn from Eretz Yisrael with her family in order to gain access to the best plastic surgeons available.

Now, as the school year approached, she faced treatments and surgeries, and on top of it all, the frightening prospect of meeting new people in a new school. Living with her mother and grandmother in Boro Park, she tried to build up strength to face the tests that lay ahead. The school that had accepted her planned to address the girls before Devora arrived, urging them to be sensitive to her and avoid staring or hurting her feelings in any way.

On the day that Devora entered the class, the girls did their best to make her feel welcome. At first, the scarring on her face was shocking to them; even with their principal's warning, they could not have imagined such disfigurement. They found it difficult to look at her. But as the weeks went by, Devora's personality emerged and the girls began to see past the exterior. She was friendly, funny, positive, and smart. Despite Devora's fears, she was becoming an accepted member of the class.

Then one afternoon during recess, Devora got into an argument with a classmate. In her fit of temper, the classmate blurted out the stinging words, "Why don't you be quiet already! You're the ugliest person anyone has ever seen!"

No sooner had the words left the girl's mouth than she knew she had done grave harm. Much as she wished she could retract the words, she could not. The damage was done, and a stunned Devora fled the scene in tears.

Devora ran home. "I'm never going back there," she told her mother. "Never!"

"I can't believe a Bais Yaakov girl could be that insensitive," her mother said. "Tomorrow, we are going back to that school and speaking to the principal and getting that girl expelled. She has no right to be there with *middos* like that."

When Devora's grandmother came home, she heard the story and her daughter's plan for redressing the wrong. While the grandmother sympathized with Devora's pain, she did not weigh in on the fate of the girl who had caused the pain. Then, later in the evening, she called Devora aside for a private conversation.

"Listen to me, Devora," she said. "If you go back to school tomorrow and get that girl kicked out, what will you accomplish? Nothing, absolutely nothing. All that will happen is that this girl will no longer have a school to go to. I have a better idea. I know you are in a lot of pain and want to get this girl back. But you and I both know that you are going to need a lot of *berachah* and *hatzlachah* in life. Even with all the operations, you will always have some scarring.

"So here is my idea. Take all the pain you have stored up within you and use it to daven to Hashem that you should find yourself a good *shidduch* when the time comes. You will have a great *zechus* to have your *tefillah* answered if you use that energy for *tefillah* instead of for revenge."

Devora was touched by the wisdom of her grandmother's words. She began to daven to Hashem, letting her tears flow freely. She begged Hashem to help her find an effective treatment, and when the time came, to help her find a good *shidduch*. She put the hurtful incident out of her mind and returned to school.

Several years later, after Devora had graduated high school and seminary, she was introduced to a great boy. He was the first boy she went out with, but he was the only one she needed to meet, for he was the right one. As she walked down the aisle at her wedding and saw her grandmother standing on the side, gazing proudly at her, she leaned over and gave her a warm hug. "It is all because of you that I am here today," she whispered. "Thank you, Bubby. I owe you everything!"

These stories illustrate that when the gates of Heaven seemed locked to a person's prayers, we have one irresistible battering ram that pushes our tefillos through. That is the power of forgiveness, for when Hashem sees His children showing compassion to those who have done them wrong, in equal measure He shows compassion to us, despite our flaws and deficiencies. Forgiveness is never surrender; it is the only real victory.

Bumper Cars

Sometimes life feels like a bumper-car ride in an amusement park. You ride along and people keep crashing into you, bumping you in this way and that way. You think they are disrupting your progress when in reality, they are bumping you into the right direction by helping you understand that you don't own the road. You have to share it and make room for others along the way. Rabbi Berger, a noted mechanech, learns that lesson in the story he tells here.*

As a *menahel* of a large yeshivah, my job is to give my hundreds of students the best *chinuch* possible. And a vital factor in reaching that goal is to hire only the best rebbeim. They must not only know how to teach, but how to instill in their students a love of learning and an appreciation of being a Jew. A second vital element is the smooth running of the school. I try to be systematic and organized, and I expect my rebbeim to do the same.

That is where my troubles began with Rabbi Bloom,* a second-grade rebbi in my yeshivah. He was a tremendously learned individual and he exuded a real enthusiasm for Torah. He was the perfect rebbi, it would seem, except that he lacked any sense of orderliness. He forgot the school rules and overlooked the things that, to me, were so important.

When the recess bell rang to call the students back to class, Rabbi Bloom would give his class extra time outdoors. "They learned so well today, they deserve it!" he would cheerfully explain. When I would walk into his classroom, his students would rarely be in their seats. Instead, they would be gathered around his desk like a flock of geese. True, they would be talking about the day's learning, but Rabbi Bloom would rile them up into an over-excited state as he tossed candies at the boys who asked good questions. Was this yeshivah, or was it camp?

I contemplated dismissing Rabbi Bloom many times but never did it because somehow, despite his unorthodox methods, his students learned. They were very successful in the subsequent grades and knew their material very well. Even boys who had struggled in other classes would suddenly experience success with Rabbi Bloom. The parents all loved him too, because their children ran off to yeshivah each day with eager anticipation. When parent-teacher night arrived, parents would go out of their way to come to me to praise Rabbi Bloom. His methods grated on my nerves, but I could not deny that he was a great rebbi.

Then one day, Rabbi Bloom crossed the line. Our yeshivah was rapidly outgrowing its facilities, and we had begun a building campaign. We were looking for a wealthy donor who was willing to sponsor this immense and costly endeavor.

A friend of mine told me about a very wealthy individual who was seeking an opportunity to donate a building in memory of his parents. This was exactly the type of situation I was hoping to find, so I quickly made contact with the potential donor, whose name was Mr. Rose.* I came to his home and spoke to him at length about our yeshivah, its philosophy, its success, and its tremendous need to expand.

"I'd like to see the place in action," he told me. We set the date of his visit for the following week.

The day before Mr. Rose was expected, I called my rebbeim to a meeting "Tomorrow, someone is coming to observe our yeshivah," I told them. "This is a crucial day for us, because this person is considering sponsoring our new building in memory of his parents. He is looking to associate their name with a yeshivah that he finds worthy, and I would like that to be our yeshivah. So please, make sure your classrooms are clean and orderly and that all the boys are on their best behavior. Our guest will be visiting every class."

The next morning at 10, Mr. Rose arrived. Everything was running smoothly when he entered the building. The halls were clear of stragglers and the classrooms were occupied with busy students and their rebbeim. We started our tour with the higher grades and worked our way down. I must say that I was proud to show him what our yeshivah was all about. In class after class, the boys were sitting in their seats, raising their hands and asking questions. The rebbeim were engaging their students in discussion.

As we neared the classrooms of the younger grades, the boys' chanting could be heard in the hallways. One class was reciting the *Chumash*. Another class was davening. Their sweet young voices created a heart-warming symphony. But then, my ears became attuned to a different sort of noise. It was laughing, banging, and shouting. As we closed in on the noise, I realized with shock and dismay that in Rabbi Bloom's class, it was business as usual. I tried to steer Mr. Rose in a different direction, but his curiosity was already aroused.

"What's going on in there?" he asked me. I was horrified by the thought of opening the door onto this little island of chaos, but I had no choice. We opened the door and saw a sight that was outrageous even by Rabbi Bloom's standards. The boys had upended their desks and sat perched atop them. They pushed the desks along like bumper cars, crashing into each other and laughing uproariously as they banged and clanged. I felt my face grow hot with embarrassment and anger. Where was Rabbi Bloom in all of this?

Then I saw him. He, too, was sitting on top of a desk, riding around the room singing a song. With each crash, he would laugh with the boys and then continue to sing. I stood there in silence, not sure of what to say. I glanced at Mr. Rose to see if I could gauge his reaction; he seemed to be amused by the sight, but I was fuming.

Later, I called Rabbi Bloom into my office. "Rabbi Bloom, what was going on here today?" I asked him.

"I made a deal with the boys that if they would finish the chapter we were learning, we would have a *siyum*. Today we finished the chapter, so we are celebrating by playing bumper cars."

"But I told you clearly yesterday that Mr. Rose would be coming to visit today. I told you that he was an important potential donor for our new building. How could you do this to me?"

"I'm really sorry. It's just that in all the excitement of finishing the chapter, I forgot about the guest."

"This is just inexcusable, Rabbi Bloom," I told him firmly. "It is no longer possible for me to have you as a rebbi in this yeshivah. I am giving you a week's notice, and you will have to find yourself another position."

"Look, Rabbi Berger, I am really sorry that I forgot about the guest, but I have 10 children at home and if I don't have this job, I have no way to support them."

"My yeshivah is my main concern," I told him. "And you are most likely the cause of us losing a million-dollar donation that we desperately need. You've caused the yeshivah great damage, and I simply cannot keep you on."

I let him know that the conversation was over, and he left my office. It wasn't an easy thing to do, but I felt strongly that I had made the correct move. Rabbi Bloom was simply not a good match for my yeshivah.

Only a few days later, strange things began to happen in my life. First, I got a frantic call from my wife reporting that my son had taken a bad fall from his bike. His leg was broken and he ended up in a cast and crutches. The very next day, my daughter was badly cut by a glass window that suddenly shattered. Soon after that, my wife tripped in the street and sprained her ankle. I realized that this flood of accidents was very out of the ordinary, and that heaven was sending me a message. But what was it?

I sought the advice of a *gadol*. When I told him what was happening to my family, he immediately asked me, "Did you recently cause pain to anyone?"

I described the entire episode of Rabbi Bloom and Mr. Rose. After hearing the story, the *gadol* told me that my actions had been wrong. The rebbi had been doing his job of teaching the class to the best of his abilities, and his actions were not a cause for his dismissal. Clearly Hashem was repaying me for the pain I had caused Rabbi Bloom. To prevent any more harm from befalling my family, I had to ask Rabbi Bloom for forgiveness and offer him his job back.

When I heard the *gadol's* advice, I was taken aback that I could have misjudged the situation so badly. I had wrongly taken the bread off a family's table. I immediately called Rabbi Bloom to express my deep regret and offer him his old job back.

Rabbi Bloom, being a good-hearted individual, forgave me right away. However, he could not come back to yeshivah, as he had already secured another position.

A week later I got a letter in the mail from Mr. Rose, along with a very large check. The content of the letter was a further awakening.

> *Dear Rabbi Berger*
>
> *I have ended my search for a yeshivah building to dedicate to my parents' memory. There were many fine yeshivos that I visited during my search and each one had great advantages. However, of all the yeshivos I saw, I felt that yours was the most worthy because of the true love the rebbeim have for their talmidim. This was most obvious to me during my trip to the second-grade class of Rabbi Bloom. Never have I seen a rebbi so attuned to his students that he was enjoying himself playing games with them. The sight of the rebbi riding around the floor with his talmidim was one that I will never forget. A yeshivah that encourages that type*

of relationship between talmid and rebbi is the right yeshivah for me. It is a most worthy investment and a zechus for the memory of my parents.

Enclosed you will find the first check to begin the building campaign.

Yours truly,
Moshe Rose

When I read this letter I was simply shocked. While I was so convinced that Rabbi Bloom had ruined our chances of getting the donation, he was in fact the major reason that we got it. This story truly changed my life because I saw how wrong I could be. Stuck in my own perspective, I was blinded to the true worth of someone like Rabbi Bloom. In my anger, I had jumped to judge him and didn't think deeply enough about the consequences of my actions. I learned from this episode that rather than disregarding people who are not the way we want them to be, we have to work on ourselves to accept them and see the unique value of their ways.

Another lesson we can learn from this story is that we never know how Hashem will bring salvation. We sometimes think the only way it will happen is if we follow a certain course of action, when in reality Hashem may have an entirely different route. Our job is to remember that Hashem is in the driver's seat.

Rescuing Hashem's Children

The following story was related by Rabbi Zecharia Wallerstein during a lecture prior to Tishah B'Av.

Walking into a shul in Bayit Vegan one morning, Yossi Roth's* eyes settled on a father and two sons seated close by. There was something distinctive about the family. They were dressed in Chassidish fashion, and all three of them had long, silky *peyos* of golden blond. Their complexions were unusually fair, and Yossi noticed that the one child who was looking his way had crystal blue eyes. Their coloring, their facial structure, and even their broad build gave Yossi the intuitive feeling that they were perhaps of German descent. If so, he wondered, how did they end up dressed in Chassidish clothing, davening in a shul in Bayit Vegan?

His curiosity was still going strong when davening was over. Yossi, who was in Israel on a visit, asked his host about the family. "You're right that they are German," his friend told him. "And they have an amazing story ..."

That father of the family, Avrohom, grew up in Germany after the war. His mother raised him alone, as his father had passed away when he was just a baby.

Avrohom attended public school and was firmly instilled with pride in his nationality. Then, he entered college. It was there that his interest in history brought him face to face with the unfathomable reality of Germany's role as perpetrator of the worst crime against humanity ever committed. As the facts became clear, Avrohom's pride turned to confusion.

He felt certain that there must have been sound reasons for the Germans' assault on the Jews. The victims could not have been the innocents they had claimed to be. Perhaps they were traitors or subversives. Avrohom devoted himself to Holocaust research, delving diligently into resource after resource until he arrived at one inescapable conclusion. The German people bore the blood of millions of innocents on their hands.

Avrohom's confusion now turned to shame. He needed to know more. He needed to comprehend, to whatever extent possible, the vast scope of this incomprehensible bout of national madness. He knew that he could not get the full story from German sources, and so, he traveled to Yad Vashem in Israel. There he uncovered even more details and gruesome truths about the depravity of the German nation. Sickened by what he learned, he decided that he could no longer be a part of that nation.

Throughout all his research, he had become attracted to Judaism and the Jewish people. In order to learn more about how the Jewish people lived their lives, he found work on a kibbutz. There, he developed a tremendous bond with Judaism, and began looking for a way to convert. His first step was to begin learning in a yeshivah for *baalei teshuvah*. There he remained for two years. When he was ready and fully certain that his commitment was sincere, he became a Jew.

Shortly after his conversion, he was introduced to Sarah, a young woman who had also converted. The two became engaged and prepared to begin a brand new life together.

During the entire time in which Avrohom's transformation had been taking place, he maintained a close tie with his mother. Naturally, he invited her to come to Israel for the wedding.

On the day of the wedding, for the first time in many years, Avrohom and his mother were able to spend time together. With the easy intimacy of mother and child, they reminisced about his childhood and spoke about the future he envisioned. At one point in their conversation, Avrohom decided to ask his mother a question that had long been on his mind.

"Mother, you never really told me how father died, and now that I'm getting married, I feel that it is only right that I know." Peering sincerely into his mother's eyes, he was quick to see her immediate discomfort at the question.

"Please son, I don't think the day of your wedding is the right time to discuss your father," she answered hesitantly. "Let's discuss it another time."

Now Avrohom's formerly dormant curiosity was sharply piqued. "No, Mother, I think we have pushed this off way too long. I want to know, how did father die?"

His mother sighed, preparing herself for a difficult mission. "There's no easy way to tell you this," she began, "but your father is alive. He is serving a life sentence in prison for his role in the Holocaust."

Avrohom sat dumbstruck, staring disbelievingly at his mother.

"During the war, your father was a Gestapo agent," she continued. "He was responsible for killing thousands of Jews. After the war, he was put on trial and was sentenced to life in prison. All your life, I didn't want you to know the bitter truth about your father."

"You are right, Mother. I don't want to hear about this on the day of my wedding," Avrohom answered in a near-whisper. "If that's who my father was, I want no part of him."

A few years passed and Avrohom's devotion to Torah and mitzvos was growing steadily. One day, as he sat learning in *kollel*, he received an urgent phone call. It was his mother.

"Son, your father is very sick and will soon be gone from this world," his mother told him. "He has asked to see you before he dies."

"I have nothing to say to him," Avrohom replied instantly. "I don't even consider him my father."

"I understand," his mother answered. "But still, he is your father who brought you into the world. Seeing you is all he's asking."

Avrohom decided that he would return to Germany to see his father, but only on the condition that he would bring his two sons along with him. He imagined the former Nazi's face as he looked upon his own descendants and saw standing before him living proof the wrongness and hopelessness of the mission to which he had devoted himself. The dying Nazi would come face to face with the living, thriving children of Avrohom.

A few days later Avrohom and his children arrived at the German prison where his father had lived out his life. They were led into a room where his father lay, pale and motionless. They were given 30 minutes alone.

The first observation Avrohom made was that, even in his father's current condition, Avrohom bore a striking resemblance to him. Father and son looked at each other in silence. Finally, Avrohom began to say what he had come to say.

"Father, I am so ashamed of my past. To think that I am the son of a Nazi! You are a murderer. You killed innocent Jews.

"Because of what you did, I had no father. I grew up alone in the world and found no peace for my soul until I embraced Judaism and found purpose in life. I am now living a life that I chose to live because it made the most sense to me in a world gone mad. My life now has meaning and the Torah has been my guide to help me understand how to live.

"Father, the Nazis have been defeated, and yet the Jewish people are thriving. No force of evil would ever be able to defeat them. Like other powers before them, the Nazis fell and the Jews remained alive and well. Father, you joined the wrong side of history and paid the price with your life."

Avrohom's father listened to his son in silence and then offered his justifications for how he was drawn into the horrendous crimes he committed. He talked about following orders and the fate that awaited those who balked. Nevertheless, he acknowledged that he had made some irreparable mistakes.

As he spoke, he gazed at the children standing before him, wondering at this strange turn of events. He, of all people, had a Jewish son and Jewish grandchildren. However, Avrohom could not mistake the look of love in his father's eyes as he studied his grandchildren's faces. Avrohom had an important question to ask, and only a few minutes left to obtain an answer.

"Father, I know that you are not pleased with my choice of becoming a Jew and you never dreamed that you would have Jewish grandchildren, but believe me, you somehow earned a very great merit in this. You are leaving behind descendants who will follow the ways of G-d. My question to you is, what did you do to deserve this? What good deed could you have done in your life to merit two beautiful Jewish grandchildren?"

"Son, there is only one incident that comes to mind that could explain it. During the war, we had invaded a town and had cleared it of Jews. We rounded up all the Jews of the town and shot them all. Whoever wasn't killed was placed on cattle-cars headed to the concentration camps. We went from house to house searching for every Jew we could find, and we found plenty of them. Of course the moment they were found, we dragged them out of hiding and shot them.

"My commander ordered me to check a barn that we had somehow overlooked. I obeyed his command and went into the barn with my gun drawn, ready to kill any Jew on sight. As I entered, I immediately saw two little frightened children hiding in a stack of hay. Only their eyes were visible. Somehow, my heart felt for these poor, scared children and I decided to make believe I didn't see them. I closed the door of the barn and let them live. When I reported back to my commander, I told him that there was no one in the barn. I believe that because I saved those two Jewish children G-d granted me two Jewish grandchildren as a reward."

Rabbi Wallerstein drew a powerful lesson for us from this story. If Hashem was willing to grant such an awesome reward — two precious Jewish grandchildren — to a Nazi who had so much blood on his hands, then how much greater is the reward for us when we make an effort to save Hashem's children. We need not be on the front lines of battle to save lives. We only have to try to encourage someone who is going through a hard time, or bring a relative or a friend closer to Hashem. By strengthening the bond between a Jew and his Creator, we save a Jewish life. At the same time, we build the *achdus and ahavas Yisrael* that brings the *geulah* that much closer.

As Avrohom in our story discovered, through the Jewish people's mourning over the destruction, they gain the merit to rebuild.

The Prince of Torah

To stay spiritually charged, a Jew has to remain in constant contact with Hashem, whether through Torah learning, performance of mitzvos or acts of chesed. If a person allows himself to become unplugged, then his spiritual batteries are in danger of a serious power outage.

One powerful image, imprinted permanently in a person's mind, can sometimes do more to inspire him than thousands of words of *mussar.* Just such an image became mine to treasure forever on one Yom Kippur spent at the Mirrer Yeshivah in Brooklyn.

The *beis midrash* was filled to capacity with hundreds of people. The sound of *tefillah* was like thunder, rumbling during some parts of the prayers, and then bursting into a dramatic roar at the climactic moments. At the head of the assemblage was Rav Shmuel Berenbaum, the Mirrer Rosh Yeshivah. I could see him from my spot in the crowd, and it was a sight I will never forget. His entire being seemed energized, his face aglow, his body consumed with the intense effort of leading his *kehillah* and himself to the great moment of Divine forgiveness.

Throughout the day I noticed Rav Shmuel repeat an unusual gesture. Each time the *chazzan* said *Kaddish*, he would raise his right fist into the air during the words *"Amen yehei sh'mei rabba."* After the first time I noticed it, I watched for it again and again, and indeed, his fist shot up and into the air vigorously, each and every time. I wondered what it meant, until during one particular *Kaddish*, when the yeshivah was literally shaking with the sound of those precious words, the reason for Rav Shmuel's action suddenly became clear to me.

"Amen yehei sh'mei rabba" was our rallying cry, and Rav Shmuel was the general, leading his troops — his yeshivah — into battle. Together, we were storming the Gates of Heaven, and he, with his fist raised into the air, was urging his troops to charge. The intensity of *tefillah* he stirred with that gesture did indeed crash through the barriers of each person's

Rav Shmuel Berenbaum

heart, and no doubt, through the Gates of Heaven as well. When I picture him standing there, his fist in the air, the image never fails to carry me up to a higher place, where my connection to Hashem is, at least for a few moments, strong and clear.

Rav Shmuel's power to move us with just his gesture, just his facial expression, sprang directly from his persona — an embodiment of the Torah and its holiness. This became even more evident at his *levayah,* when dozens of speakers attempted to capture with words the full glory of a man who was beyond description. One story, however, conveyed to me a glimpse of his true essence.

The Rosh Yeshivah's son Rav Asher related that his father endured a great deal of suffering during his final illness. Despite painful treatments and medications that drained the energy from him, his fiery *neshamah* kept burning. He would carry on as well as possible, giving his *shiurim* and engaging in his own learning with all the strength left in him.

Eventually, however, his physical limitations caught up with him. He became bedridden, and his mind became clouded with weakness and pain. Even then, he asked his son to speak to him in learning so that in his final days on earth, he could continue to engage his mind in Torah. One day, when even that became too much for him, he told his son, "I want you to repeat with me the *sheish mitzvos temidios* (the six constant mitzvos)."

Speaking was a great strain on the Rosh Yeshivah at this point, but nevertheless, his son did as he was asked. He named the first mitzvah and his father repeated it. He named the second mitzvah, and his father repeated that one as well. They continued in this fashion until all six had been recited. Having fulfilled his father's request, the son asked, "Tatte, why did you insist on repeating the *sheish mitzvos?"*

The Rosh Yeshivah answered, "My son, all my life I have been able to be immersed in Torah. It is my lifeline, my connection to Hashem. But now, my head is weak and I am unable to concentrate in learning. But I still need to be connected to Hashem. By repeating the *sheish mitzvos,* I am staying connected."

The Prince of Torah left us with a legacy: to forever remain connected.

Chapter 4:

Chesed

With All Your Heart

A Real Lifesaver

The Chofetz Chaim says in sefer Ahavas Chesed that when the scales are balanced between good and evil and your life is hanging in the balance, kindness has the power to tip the scales in your favor and counterbalance all evil. Sometimes the merit of your kindness is stored away for years and can be a real lifesaver when you need it most.

Simon* was born and raised in Russia with only the barest knowledge of his Jewish roots. When he came to America and settled in Minneapolis, he found his heart being drawn to Judaism and began to explore his heritage. The more he learned, the more he wanted to learn, and so he joined a local shul and embarked on his quest in earnest. He began davening regularly and attending various *shiurim* that were offered throughout the week.

The *shiur* that really grabbed his heart was one on the Chofetz Chaim's *sefer Ahavas Chesed*, which taught about the power of kindness. There, Simon learned that kindness to others was one of the foundations upon which the world stood, and a counterbalance on the heavenly scales that can outweigh one's sins and save one's life. The image of this scale, tipped in favor of life by a kind act, became one of Simon's life themes.

At the time that Simon joined the shul, a young man in the community was suffering from grave health problems. Simon, guided by the Chofetz Chaim's advice, mounted a major campaign to raise money for the sick young man's care. He added a substantial amount of his own money to the fund and was able to remove at least some of the worries from the man's overburdened heart.

That was the first of Simon's many *chesed* ventures. He became the go-to man when help was needed, but he did not wait to be asked. He searched for opportunities to lend his willing hands to any situation. When anyone asked him about his non-stop *chesed*, he would tell them about the counterbalance that could tip the scales in his favor.

On a Wednesday evening, August 2, 2007, Simon was driving his car across the interstate bridge. The span was loaded with bumper-to-bumper traffic when a scene of surreal horror began to unfold. There was a loud bang and the bridge began to shake and gyrate wildly Suddenly, the roadbed folded like a toy. Dust and smoke shot far up into the sky while the cars — including Simon's — plunged 100 feet into the raging waters of the Mississippi River.

Panic-stricken drivers were trapped in their vehicles as they sank into the water. Simon watched helplessly as the dark, chilly water seeped into his car. The end had come. He closed his eyes and began to say the *Shema*. Then, running on nothing but adrenalin and instinct, he opened his seat belt and crawled to the door. He pulled the handle to release the latch, but when he pushed the door, it would not budge. The water pressure pushed back with much more force than Simon could possibly muster.

In the midst of the noise and chaos, there was another ear-splitting crash. A metal bridge girder had plunged from on-high and crashed through his rear window. Now the water gushed in and the car began to sink. In desperation, Simon tried the door again and this time, miraculously, it opened. He maneuvered his way out of the car and began swimming for his life, alert to the falling debris and jagged flotsam all around him. Rescue workers were already on the scene, and in moments, he found himself sitting safe and sound in a rescue boat, amazed to be alive.

The rescue workers carried Simon to an ambulance and he was rushed to the hospital, which had turned into a crowded triage center flooded with victims of the disaster. Simon had emerged with only a few minor injuries.

Soon a team of investigators arrived to interview the survivors, seeking evidence of what went wrong A bridge engineer came to speak with Simon, who described his amazing escape.

"You know that you are a living miracle," the engineer told him. "There was really no way that you could have escaped that submerged car. You would never have been able to open that door on your own, because there was probably a thousand pounds of water pressure against the car door. Nobody could have opened that door.

"But I think what happened was this: When the back window was smashed by the metal girder and water started to gush in, the water pressure on the inside of your car equalized with the pressure on the outside. At that moment when you pushed the door, your little push tipped the balance scale in your favor."

When Simon heard the engineer say that the scales were balanced and that his action had "tipped the scale," a chill went down his spine. He immediately realized that the merit of his acts of kindness had tipped the scale and saved his life.

The Chofetz Chaim's words were no longer just a theme to Simon. They told the true story of his own, personal miracle.

As sefer Ahavas Chesed points out, the real beneficiary of an act of chesed is the giver.

Warmed by Her Heart

Do you ever think about how far an act of kindness can go? You may do some small favor, say a few kind words, make a quick phone call, and think your deed was barely a "blip" on the radar screen. But for the recipient, the impact could be life-changing. An act of kindness, no matter how small, will forever be remembered in Heaven and on earth.

The ultimate wellspring of wisdom and kindness, Rebbetzin Kanievsky's life was a rich tapestry woven of the thousands of people she uplifted. When she passed from this world, they flocked to her home to comfort her bereaved family and to bring to light some of the previously unknown episodes that comprised her great legacy.

Here is the story shared by a woman who was one of the many *baalei teshuvah* the Rebbetzin inspired:

One morning, I came to pray with the Rebbetzin at the sunrise *minyan* she customarily attended. I knew I would find her there, and that being in her presence as she prayed would help me to move forward on my path of *teshuvah*. I had reached a certain point at which I felt stuck. I knew I wanted more, but I wasn't ready for the next level of commitment.

I found her, as I knew I would. We davened and then began to say some *Tehillim*. Although the atmosphere was so pure and beautiful, I could not concentrate as I would have wanted to, because the early morning air was raw and cold. I felt it all the way down into my bones, but I tried not to betray my discomfort in front of the Rebbetzin. I shivered on the inside, while on the outside, I just kept my eyes on my *Tehillim*.

All of a sudden, I saw the Rebbetzin get up and quietly walk out of the women's section. A few minutes later, she returned with a hot-water bottle in her hand. She motioned to me to come and sit in the seat next to her, and so I did. I took the seat right by her side.

Without saying a word, she simply placed the hot-water bottle on top of my freezing cold feet. Then she took my icy hands into her warm ones, and rubbed my hands until the chill was gone from them. Not only my hands and feet, but my entire being, felt enveloped in a blanket of warmth. The obstacle that blocked my soul from complete *teshuvah* melted that day into an innocuous puddle. I returned to Hashem with all my heart, all in the merit of the Rebbetzin.

I will never forget that touch of warmth.

Another *baalas teshuvah* related the following story:

After I became a *chozer b'teshuvah,* there were many areas of my life that were confusing for me. The Rebbetzin was the adviser I sought out most often. There was one situation that was particularly serious, and when I came to her for direction, she consulted with her husband, Rav Chaim Kanievsky, and passed along his advice to me. "When the problem is resolved," she said, "come back and let me know."

Baruch Hashem, I followed the Rav's advice and a few months later, my problem was resolved just as he said it would be. It was time to report back to the Rebbetzin. I asked my sister, who was not religious, to accompany me to Bnei Brak to meet the Rebbetzin and receive a *berachah* from her. She was reluctant — rebbetzins and *berachos* were not within her comfort zone. However, I convinced her that this Rebbetzin was so warm and accepting that she would certainly not feel awkward. On the contrary, she would feel a real uplift. Finally, she agreed to come along.

When we got to the Rebbetzin's house, we found out that she was in shul davening. I took my sister and set out toward the shul to try to meet her there, but as we approached, I saw her already heading back to her house. She was surrounded by a group of women who accompanied her. As I approached with my sister, the women noticed her mode of dress, which marked her clearly as non-religious. They stepped aside and let us into the inner circle, perhaps believing that my sister, like so many other women, had come for help in doing *teshuvah.*

I spoke first. I reminded the Rebbetzin of our conversation several months earlier and reported that the situation had been resolved. She greeted the news with sincere happiness, clearly recalling our conversation and my problem — one of dozens she hears each day.

When we finished our brief conversation, I introduced the Rebbetzin to my sister. She looked at my sister with pure love and warmth, seeing nothing other than a young Jewish woman with a pure Jewish soul. This was born out by the *berachah* she gave: "You should soon marry a *tzaddik* and a G-d-fearing man."

I could see by my sister's gentle smile that she was touched by the Rebbetzin's warm words. These were not traits she had ever considered seeking in a husband, but the Rebbetzin obviously felt that she was worthy of such a man.

Suddenly, one of the women who was standing with the group turned to my sister and in a loud, sharp tone of voice said, "How dare you come to see the Rebbetzin dressed like that!"

My sister's face turned pale, and tears of humiliation sprang to her eyes. She stood there like an actor caught in the spotlight, struggling to remember the lines. The Rebbetzin went directly over to the woman who had screamed, and spoke to her for a few moments until she calmed down. Then, she came to my sister and wrapped her in a comforting hug. There she remained, soothing my sister until she stopped crying.

At that point, she announced to the women around her, "I want you all to come over to this special woman here and receive a *berachah* from her. She has a very special merit, for she was insulted, and she restrained herself from returning the insult to the one who scorned her. She thus has the merit to give *berachos.*"

The woman all lined up in front of my sister, an irreligous woman and asked her for a *berachah*. At first, my sister was dumbfounded by the situation in which she found herself. Her? Giving out blessings to these women? But then she realized that, at this propitious moment, she really had the power to help them. She began blessing each and every one with her full heart. Because of the Rebbetzin's wisdom and incredible love for each Jewish soul, my irreligious sister was transformed, for those few minutes, into a rebbetzin. Her honor was restored, her insulted heart was healed, and every woman standing there had the opportunity to witness firsthand the superhuman power of true holiness.

One way to guide our own steps in the right direction is to ask ourselves, "What will people remember about me when, at the age of 120, I leave the world." If we think about this, we will never ignore an opportunity to help another person, and we will build a lasting legacy of kindness.

A Well-Nourished Soul

There are people who eat like princes, yet always feel empty and wanting. There are people who sustain themselves on very little, yet always feel satiated. Obviously, the amount of food a person consumes is not always the true measure of nourishment, as this story of two cousins trapped in Auschwitz so eloquently proves.

Yossi had promised himself that he would live. The Nazis had erased so much of his family, so much of his world, but he was determined to some day rebuild it all. But that required surviving, and surviving required food.

Day by day, he felt himself fading into an oblivious fog. It would only take one moment of weakness — one instance of buckling knees or lost balance — to provoke a guard to end his life with a bullet thoughtlessly delivered at point-blank range. He had seen it so many times in Auschwitz that it had almost become mundane. He had to find a way to get some food before it was too late.

It was nighttime. The only sounds Yossi heard were the labored breathing of his fellow inmates who had sunken into sleep. Listening carefully for the footsteps of guards in the vicinity of the barracks, Yossi slipped out of his bed and moved silently to the door. In a moment, he was outside, peering in every direction, straining for the glint of a flashlight or soft thump of approaching boots. Staying in the shadows, sliding noiselessly across the camp toward the kitchen, he at last found the treasure he was seeking — the dumpster.

Yossi began digging for anything edible. It didn't matter what it was, just as long as it could still the hunger pangs in his stomach and give him some strength. Quickly and carefully, he sifted through the contents of the dumpster, but he found nothing. There were no leftovers in Auschwitz.

Suddenly, Yossi heard movement. His heart leapt in fear. He had been caught! But when he turned his head toward the sound, he saw that there was no Nazi standing behind him. There was a boy his own age: his cousin Moishe.

"What are you doing here?" Yossi whispered.

"I'm starving, Yossi," said Moishe, his voice hoarse with exhaustion. "I can't take it any more. I figured I'd take a chance and see if I could find something to eat in here."

"Oy, Moishe, you and I had the same idea. But I've gone through every bit of garbage in there and there is nothing to eat. Let's get back to our barracks before we get caught."

"There's got to be something in there!" Moishe protested. "I don't care what it is. I can't take it any more. I can't go on."

"I know, Moishe. I'm hungry too. I wish there was something in there for us, but there isn't. Let's go."

Moishe began to weep softly. "Please, Yossi, give me some food. Please ..."

Witnessing the fear and desperation that was overcoming his cousin, Yossi's heart broke. He wished more than anything that he could reach into his pocket and pull out a piece of bread to give him. But alas, he had nothing to give. Except his love.

Yossi embraced his cousin and Moishe wept on his shoulder. "I don't have food to give you," Yossi said softly into his ear. "But I'm here for you, and anything I can do to help you survive this war, I'm going to do. We're in it together, and we're walking out of here together, too."

Fifty years had passed. Both Yossi and Moishe survived the war and emigrated to Eretz Yisrael, where they each married and raised children and grandchildren. Their families led lives of Torah and mitzvos, fulfilling the men's dream of rebuilding what the Nazis had attempted to erase forever.

When Yossi passed away, Moishe came to comfort his bereaved family. He sat in the *shivah* house and cried like one of the mourners. For decades, the survivors had pushed aside memories of the death camp in order to fully engage in life. But now, the time had come to share with Yossi's family the legacy of greatness their father left behind.

"We were 12 when we were taken to Auschwitz," Moishe began. "I was a lost soul. So frightened, so hungry, so lonely. If it hadn't been for your father, I would never have made it. I wouldn't be here today, and neither of course would any of my children or grandchildren. We all owe our lives to your father."

"What did he do for you that saved your life?" one of Yossi's children asked. They had always known that their father's story was far more dramatic than the few broad facts he had been willing to share. Now they would discover some pieces of the real picture.

Moishe told the story of the dumpster. "You have to understand," he said, "I was at the edge of my endurance. My heart was ready to explode. But your father did something I would never forget. He gave me a hug. And that hug warmed my soul, stopped my hunger pains and saved my life.

"There were many times in the coming months when I wanted to give up. I was ready to die and join the rest of my family, but then I recalled that hug. While we did backbreaking work without any food to give us strength, I wanted to collapse, but then I recalled that hug. When we were taken on a death march, I just wanted to drop in my place and let them shoot me, but I recalled the feeling of that hug. And throughout my whole life, whenever I was feeling hopeless, I remembered that hug and strengthened myself."

Moishe recounted many more stories of Yossi's early years. He gave the children a view of their father that they had never been granted during his life — a view of a man who was even greater than they already had known him to be. At last, the hour grew late and Moishe got up to leave.

"Please eat something before you go," said one of the children. "You've been sitting here all night and you haven't eaten a thing!"

"Oh, no thanks. I'm not even hungry," Moishe replied.

"But you haven't eaten in hours!" the son replied.

"Well, it's a strange thing, but ever since the time your father gave me that hug in Auschwitz, I never really needed to eat much to be full. I guess that hug was enough to fill me up."

When you have nothing concrete to give another person to assist him in a time of need, you still have a powerful way to alleviate his troubles. Your empathy, love, and compassion can act as a salve for his problems, and provide comfort that lasts a lifetime.

A Heart of Gold

Chesed is an act of kindness done for a friend in need. "Ahavas chesed" goes one giant step further. The Chofetz Chaim defines this sterling trait as the seeking of opportunities to help others. A person who bears this trait treats others as if they were his own sons or daughters, for whose welfare he would go above and beyond normal efforts. Rav Nosson Tzvi Finkel, the Rosh Yeshivah of Mir Yerushalayim, was the epitome of ahavas chesed. Indeed, he had a heart of gold.

Rav Nosson Tzvi Finkel started his life as a day-school student in Chicago, and ended it as the legendary Rosh Yeshivah of Mir Yerushalayim, the wellspring of Torah learning that flows out to the entire world. In the remarkable decades of his career, he became a venerated *gadol* in the world of Torah. His influence lives on in the tens of thousands of *talmidim* whom he nurtured at the Mir. Yet the Torah that occupied his mind did not exist in the intellect alone. It pervaded his heart as well, imbuing him with fine-tuned sensitivity to the needs of his fellow Jew. In this way, his legacy as a man of *chesed* lives vibrantly alongside his stature as a *gadol hador.*

Rav Nosson Tzvi Finkel

In the weeks following Rav Nosson Tzvi's passing, after a long and heroic battle with Parkinson's disease, many former *talmidim* gathered in *batei midrash* and shuls across the country to commemorate and eulogize their beloved Rosh Yeshivah. At one such gathering at Yeshiva Gedolah of Teaneck, Rabbi Mordechai Grunwald, the executive director of the Mir, told a story that embodied the *ahavas chesed* that coursed through the Rosh Yeshivah's veins.

About 15 years ago, the Rosh Yeshivah received the sad news that a close *talmid* who had been battling a critical illness had at last succumbed. The *talmid* left behind a large family, and the widow would now face the difficult challenge of serving as both mother and father to her children. Her plight burdened the Rosh Yeshivah's heart, for not only would she face the immense financial responsibilities of raising her family, but she would shoulder alone the awesome burden of keeping them on the right path. To whom could she turn for advice in their *chinuch*? Who would take an interest in their progress? Who would provide money for the extras or even the necessities that she could not afford?

The Rosh Yeshivah decided that the answer to all those questions would be — Rav Nosson Tzvi Finkel. Even though the family did not live in Eretz Yisrael, he would care for his *talmid's* widow and orphans. He would provide shelter from the storm. Thus began a decades-long commitment to the welfare of this family. To ensure that their needs did not become lost in the hectic agenda of the Rosh Yeshivah's life, he kept a picture of them in his pocket. He would call the family regularly to check on the children's progress. He helped their mother make decisions regarding schools, yeshivos, and other life decisions. He prayed for them as he prayed for his own children.

So that the children could feel his fatherly presence in their lives, the Rosh Yeshivah would regularly write letters to the boys of the family. Because of his Parkinson's, writing the letters by hand required painstaking effort. Nonetheless, to forge the warmest possible personal connection, he forced his hand and took the time to perform this arduous labor of love. His letters would be filled with Torah insights and words of encouragement, and the children would write back, sharing the *divrei Torah* they had learned in yeshivah. As they grew older, some went to Eretz Yisrael to learn, and they found an open door at Rav Nosson Tzvi's home. They were invited for a meal each week, and knew that they always had a place to go for warmth, encouragement, and advice.

Not only did the Rosh Yeshivah usher his surrogate children lovingly through their formative years, but like a true father, he loved them and cared for their welfare throughout his entire life. It was never a "case closed" — a need that was perceived, attended to, and finished. The Rosh Yeshivah's *ahavas chesed* fostered a continuous desire to give these children — even in adulthood — the benefits of fatherly love.

After Rabbi Grunwald finished his eulogy, a young man from the yeshivah approached him.

"There's another part to this story," he told Rabbi Grunwald. "I happen to know that in that family, there was a girl who was 8 years old at the time her father passed away. Because she couldn't take part in the *divrei Torah* going back and forth between Rav Nosson Tzvi and her brothers, she felt as though she were being overlooked. She longed to have the loving connection with this father figure, just as her brothers did. One day, the little girl expressed her pain to her mother, who knew exactly what to do.

"The mother called the Rosh Yeshivah and told him about her little girl's hurt feelings. He assured her that he would take care of the situation. A few days later, a letter came in the mail from Eretz Yisrael. It bore the Rosh Yeshivah's distinctive handwriting, but this time, the letter was addressed to the little girl. As soon as she saw the letter, the girl grabbed it and ran with it into her room to open it in private.

"Inside the envelope was a folded paper. She carefully removed it and unfolded it. To her utter delight, the paper was inscribed with a hand-drawn heart, within which was written a warm, loving message, signed by Rav Nosson Tzvi. She took that letter and pressed it close to her heart. She treasured that letter every day of her life.

"Now, you might wonder how I have this piece of inside information. Well, today that little girl is my wife, and I know firsthand that right up to today, that letter means the world to her."

Rav Nosson Tzvi's golden heart provided a lifetime's worth of warmth and solace to an orphaned girl.

Never Alone

In the following story related by Rabbi Duvi Bensoussan, we learn the extent of a father's love for his children, and through that, the nature of Hashem's love for us. Even in our darkest hour, Hashem is by our side, sharing our pain and suffering.

Among the many ways that Rabbi Yechiel Bornstein* served Hashem, *kiruv* was especially close to his heart. Although he was a busy, sought-after Rav of a community in Flatbush, the Shabbos table in his apartment on Ocean Parkway was the destination for many *baalei teshuvah* over the years. With his warmth, insight, and open heart, he was the perfect ambassador for Hashem's Torah.

On one Shabbos evening, Rabbi Bornstein was hosting a young man named Arik. This Russian Jew had recently discovered his heritage, and had already taken upon himself Shabbos observance, kashrus, and *tefillin*. Rabbi Bornstein was delighted to bring him into his home and share an uplifting Shabbos with him.

It was a small, intimate group around the table. The Rabbi sat at the head, with his wife and son on his right and Arik on his left. The conversation, *zemiros,* and *divrei Torah* flowed as the group partook of the delicious food Mrs. Bornstein had prepared. So warm and enjoyable was the meal that no one noticed how late the hour had become. As they prepared to *bentch,* Rabbi Bornstein glanced at his watch.

"I can't believe it's already midnight," he said. "Arik, where did you say you lived?"

"Brighton Beach," he replied, referring to a neighborhood several miles away.

"I didn't realize you would have to walk so far," the Rabbi said. "I feel terrible that we kept you here so late, and I really don't want you to walk all that way at this time of night. Why don't you sleep here and you can walk home in the morning, or if you want, stay for Shabbos and we will get you a ride afterward."

Arik wasn't hard to convince. He agreed to stay, but the question was, where in the small apartment would he sleep? Rabbi Bornstein answered the question before it was asked. "You can sleep in my son Chaim's room," he told Arik. "He is glad to give it up for the night."

This was news to Chaim. "Tatty, where will I sleep?" he asked.

"Don't worry Chaim, we will work it out. Now you go and prepare the room for Arik."

Chaim dutifully did as his father asked, all the while silently brooding about the imposition his father and their guest were making on him. Chaim finished the task and came back to the dining room to tell Arik that the room was ready.

"Thank you very much, Chaim" he responded gratefully. "Good night." He entered Chaim's room, closed the door behind him and settled in for a good night's sleep. Meanwhile, Chaim had no such comfort. He confronted his father.

"Tatty, I don't understand how you could give up my room without even asking me. You know I didn't volunteer to give it up."

"Chaim, what is the problem?" Rabbi Bornstein responded. "You'll sleep on the sofa in the living room. How many times have you fallen asleep on the sofa?"

"I can't sleep a whole night on the sofa," Chaim complained. "It's so old and the springs are all sticking out."

"You know, Chaim you are right," Rabbi Bornstein told his son. "Don't sleep on the couch. Instead, I want you to sleep on the living room floor."

"What?" Chaim asked incredulously.

"You heard me," said Rabbi Bornstein. His tone left no more room for argument. "I want you to sleep on the floor. Now go get a blanket and a pillow and go to sleep."

Grumbling under his breath, Chaim went to the linen closet to find enough pillows and blankets to cushion the hard wooden floor. He made himself a little nest of blankets and crawled inside, trying to find a comfortable position. As he lay there trying to fall asleep, he ruminated on the evening's turn of events. How did he end up on the floor while a stranger slept soundly in his bed? He tossed and turned and thought, unable to relax.

Suddenly, he heard his mother closing the door of her room and quietly walking over to him. "Chaim," she whispered. "Go sleep in my room tonight and I will sleep on the couch."

"Really, Mommy? Thank you so much ..."

"Absolutely not!" Rabbi Bornstein's voice announced firmly from the other room. "Chaim has to sleep on the floor tonight and that is final."

Chaim finally gave in to his fate, turned over on his blanket and tried to sleep. It seemed like only a few minutes later when he heard his father's voice. "Chaim, wake up," he called. "Time to get up for shul!" Chaim opened his sleepy eyes to face a new day.

"I hope you were able to sleep," Rabbi Bornstein said.

"Well, no, Tatty, I didn't sleep much at all. The floor was so uncomfortable," Chaim replied.

"Well, it's just one night. You'll catch up with your sleep, and meanwhile, you did a really big mitzvah saving Arik from a long, dangerous walk late at night."

Chaim was still irritable as he dressed for shul. "Just one night," he repeated to himself. "That's easy for you to say, Tatty. You slept in a nice comfortable bed." But he kept his thoughts to himself, for there was no point in arguing any further. What was done was done Arik stayed the rest of the day, and when Shabbos was over, Rabbi Bornstein drove him home. The matter was never mentioned again.

Twenty years later, Chaim was a married man with a large family of his own. One day, he was sitting at a meeting in his office when he was called out for an emergency phone call. "Chaim, come to the hospital right away!" his mother urged. Her voice was shaking. "It's Tatty. It doesn't look good. Please hurry!"

Rabbi Bornstein had been in the hospital already for several weeks. He was very ill, and now, it seemed that his time had come. Chaim dashed to the hospital and found his mother by his father's bedside. He came close to his father, letting him know that he was there.

"Chaim, come here, hold my hand," said Rabbi Bornstein. His voice was a labored whisper. "Son, I want you to know something. My entire life, I have always tried my best to raise you correctly. And I know that there were times when you didn't understand why I did some things, but I want you to know that whatever I did, I did it because I loved you more then anything in the world. And I wanted to teach you the right way."

Soon after these words were spoken, Chaim said the *Shema* with his father, and his father passed away. Chaim and his mother burst into tears. The moment was not unexpected, but when it occurred, the acute sense of loss ripped into their hearts. Rabbi Bornstein was really gone from this world, and they would never again be able to bask in his warmth and wisdom.

When Chaim regained his composure, he was left with a question. "Ma, what did Tatty mean when he said that I may not have understood what he was doing?"

"Chaim, your father made me promise to never tell you, but now I believe you can be told," his mother said. "About twenty years ago, we had a guest over for a Friday night meal, and Tatty offered him your bed. Do you remember that, Chaim?"

Chaim remembered the episode well.

"Well, when I went into the room for the night, I was shocked to find Tatty lying on the floor. I asked him, 'What in the world are you doing sleeping on the floor? Go to your bed!' And he gave me the most amazing answer. 'If my son is sleeping on the floor, then I will sleep on the floor. What kind of father would I be if I were to sleep in a comfortable bed while I make my son sleep on the floor? Yes, I made Chaim give up his bed to teach him *hachnasas orchim,* but I must share in his pain.'

"When your father told me that, I immediately came to offer you my bed so that at least your father would then agree to sleep in his bed. But he wouldn't hear of it. He wanted to teach you, my son, and that is why he did what he did."

> *Rabbi Bensoussan concludes: Throughout our bitter exile, in the most difficult of times, Hashem says "You are not alone. I am here with you in your pain." Just as a father could not bear to watch his son suffer alone, Hashem is by our side through everything we must endure.*

A Blanket of Warmth

When we spread a blanket of warmth on a fellow Jew in need, it not only affects the present, but can make an impact for many years to come, as the following story illustrates.

How could such an intelligent woman make such a terrible mistake? Rabbi May* held a warm, polite, and articulate letter in his hand, signed by the mother of his student, Ephraim Norman. After many discussions between them, Mrs. Norman had made her decision. She would not be re-enrolling her son in yeshivah for the coming year. Now, he had Mrs. Norman on the phone to try one last time to change her mind.

She spoke with the kind of unflappable, calm authority that left little room for argument. "Rabbi May, I appreciate all that you have done for my son and me over the years," she said, "but my decision is final. I feel that my son will gain much more in a public school than he can possibly gain in a few late-afternoon hours of secular studies at yeshivah. We have to prepare him for the future!"

"But Mrs. Norman, your son is only in the fifth grade," Rabbi May responded. "He has just begun to have the capacity to really learn Torah and appreciate it. Besides, do you know who his rebbi will be next year? It's Rabbi Shainer,* a rebbi whom everyone loves. Parents fight to get their kids into his class. He's one of the best and most caring rebbeim in our yeshivah, and Ephraim will miss having this wonderful influence in his life."

Rabbi May might as well have been talking to himself. The child's mother could see nothing beyond the path she had paved for her son, and no detours were permitted. "He could be the greatest rebbi in the world," she answered. "I'm sure he is. But does that make up for all the areas of study my son will be missing by staying in yeshivah? Does that get him into a good college and set him up for a good livelihood?

"Please, Rabbi May, I have nothing but warm feelings toward your yeshivah. Let's leave it that way and stop this discussion. Besides, I still want to help with the yeshivah Shabbaton. As I told you, I can help find hosts for the rebbeim who are going to be staying in town."

"Great, Mrs. Norman, I will let the principal know and we'll be in touch."

Rabbi Avi May, a dedicated rebbi at Yeshivah Toras Simcha,* had developed a close relationship with the Norman family when Ephraim was a student in his class. He had seen a spark in Ephraim, a real enthusiasm for Torah and mitzvos that was just waiting to catch fire. The idea of this beautiful *neshamah* being immersed in public school and the secular culture that saturated the very walls there made Rabbi May want to break down in tears. It was like watching helplessly from shore while a child drowned.

The trouble with trying to change Mrs. Norman's mind was that her decision was not emotional — it was strictly practical, based on her assessment of what would best serve her child. In fact, she expressed nothing but warmth and gratitude to the yeshivah. That is why she offered to arrange Shabbos hospitality.

The week after Rabbi May's conversation with Mrs. Norman, the Shabbaton took place. The students would enjoy a grand Friday night *seudah* together at the yeshivah. The rebbeim would all be there, and those from out of town were instructed to go to the Norman home first to find out which family would be hosting them. Thus, that Erev Shabbos was a pleasantly hectic one for the Normans.

Among the couples arriving at the Norman's were Rabbi Shainer and his wife. No sooner had Mrs. Norman greeted them than Mrs. Shainer took a step back, looked Mrs. Norman up and down and said, "Julie Karmen, is that you?"

"You do look familiar, Mrs. Shainer," said Mrs. Norman. "But where do I know you from?"

"Don't you remember me?" she replied. "I was your mother's friend. I used to come over to your house when you were a little girl."

Julie Norman looked again at the smiling face of Mrs. Shainer and in a flash of recognition, a whole dramatic episode of her childhood came rushing to the fore.

"Mrs. Shainer! Rabbi Shainer! How could I ever forget you?" she exclaimed.

Mrs. Norman had first met Rabbi and Mrs. Shainer 20 years earlier when she was a child of 8. Her family had recently moved from Israel to America so that one of her siblings could receive desperately needed medical treatment. The family landed in Brooklyn with barely enough money to rent an apartment. Food was scarce and furniture was non-existent. But the family's dire situation remained largely unknown to the neighbors. All they knew was that a sweet young family had moved in under difficult circumstances — but were those circumstances any more difficult than those of the many other struggling young families in the community?

On a Thursday afternoon shortly after the Karmen family's arrival, their neighbor, Mrs. Shainer, arrived at the apartment door with a home-baked welcome cake. When Mrs. Karmen opened the door and found her neighbor standing there, her first instinct was to stand in a position that would obstruct the view to the inside. She didn't want anyone to see how her family was living.

After a few moments of friendly small-talk, the apartment's smoke alarm began beeping in an ear-splittingly shrill tone. A flustered Mrs. Karmen dashed into the kitchen where she had left a pan of oil heating up on the stove. Without thinking, she pulled the lid off the pan and a splash of hot oil bubbled up from the pan onto her face. Her scream of pain drew Mrs. Shainer into the apartment, where she found her neighbor standing at the sink splashing cold water onto her face.

"Don't worry," she soothed Mrs. Karmen. "It's all going to be all right. I'll call Hatzolah and we'll get you some help. I'll stay with the children and you and your husband can go to the hospital." Mrs. Shainer remained there with her neighbor, trying to keep her calm. She called Mr. Karmen to come home from work, and soon, Hatzolah was taking the couple to the hospital.

With the immediate emergency tended to, Mrs. Shainer began to look around at the apartment to see what needed to be done. What she saw truly broke her heart. The only furniture was a few folding chairs and a small table. There was no couch, no dining-room table and not even any beds. The children slept on blankets spread out on the floor, and the infant was put to sleep on a baby blanket tucked away in the corner of the room. The refrigerator and pantry were empty, and the children, who now gathered around her in fear and confusion, wore ragged hand-me-downs. Mrs. Shainer was overcome with a desire to sit them all down to a plentiful, hot meal.

Her first step was to call her husband and get him on board to help. "You cannot believe how this poor family is living, right here in the middle of our community," she told him. "We need to get people to help them"

Rabbi Shainer did not need to hear another word. He called a friend on the block and together, they began gathering funds and household items to make a respectable home for the Karmen family. Beds were purchased for every member of the family, as well as a new crib for the baby. The neighbors supplied a table, dining-room chairs, and a couch. Then they went to work filling up the fridge and pantry with all the staples a young family needs. Overnight, the bare apartment was transformed into a clean, attractive, well-supplied home.

When the Karmens returned home from the hospital, they opened the door onto a whole new existence. The cloud of deprivation was lifted, and the spirits of everyone in the family, from the baby to the father, shone with happiness. They could not think of any way to express their thanks to the Shainers for what they had done. But in 8-year-old Julie's mind, the memory of their kindness was filed away in a special place of love and gratitude.

After Shabbos, Mrs. Norman called Rabbi May and told him the entire story of her encounter with Rabbi Shainer.

"I have changed my mind after all," she said. "It would be the greatest honor in the world for my son Ephraim to learn under someone as special as Rabbi Shainer. I am keeping him in yeshivah."

Ephraim stayed in yeshivah the following year and every year thereafter. He thrived under Rabbi Shainer, and remained a true *ben Torah*, all because of the warm blanket of kindness that the Shainers had spread over his mother's family, so many years ago.

On one Chol HaMoed Pesach, Rabbi Michel Twerski, the Hornosteipler Rebbe of Milwaukee, came to Lakewood and addressed hundreds of boys who had gathered in Bais Faiga Hall, where they took part in "The Greater Adventure," an hour-long learning program. He told the boys a story that teaches the long-lasting effect of an act of kindness.

When I was of bar mitzvah age, my family had the honor of hosting the Ponovezher Rav in our home. Taking advantage of this rare opportunity to spend time with a legendary *gadol,* we asked him to share some stories of the *gedolim* he had been privileged to know. Of the many engrossing stories he told, this one really made a lasting impact on me:

On one of his many fundraising trips for his yeshivah, the Rav found himself in the home of a wealthy man who had a very special quality about him. The Rav noticed that his character seemed very refined, and he exuded a true love of Torah and reverence for those devoted to learning. The man seemed to sincerely feel that in donating money to the yeshivah, he was getting the better end of the deal.

The Ponovezher Rav, after spending some time in discussion with the man, could not help but express his positive impression.

"What influenced you to reach such a high spiritual level?" he asked.

"Ponovezher Rav, you are a *talmid* of the Chofetz Chaim? I am also a *talmid* of the Chofetz Chaim. When I was a *bachur,* I was accepted into the Radin Yeshivah for the Elul *z'man*, but I was ill at the time and was not able to come to Radin until after Succos. When I came to the yeshivah with my father, we went immediately to the Chofetz Chaim to find out where I would be sleeping. The Chofetz Chaim's face turned pale.

"'Oy!' he exclaimed. 'I forgot that you were coming. All the beds have been given out already to the other students in yeshivah.'

"The Chofetz Chaim suggested that I stay in his home and sleep on an extra bench in his room until something more suitable could be found. I stayed in Radin, continuing with this arrangement, and my father went back home.

"I remember that I couldn't fall asleep that night. I was so homesick. I missed my family all the more because I was sleeping in a place where I really didn't belong, on a hard, uncomfortable bench. I tossed and turned all night long.

"At some point in the night, I heard the door of the room open and I assumed it was the Chofetz Chaim. I made believe that I was sleeping already, because I didn't want to make him feel bad. I heard the Chofetz Chaim say to himself, 'Maybe he is cold,' referring to me. He started looking around the room for something warm to cover me with. When he couldn't find an extra blanket, he said, 'I will cover him with my *ruck*' (the long coat customarily worn by the Jews of Lita)."

"That night, I slept under the Chofetz Chaim's coat while he remained without it. I still feel myself covered by the coat of the Chofetz Chaim."

Rabbi Twerski concluded the story with its lesson for us today. "We live in a cold world, a world of indifference and apathy. We can take our coat and spread it over people to warm their hearts. Sometimes this warm coat can be a smile or a friendly hello.

Sometimes it can be financial help for someone in need. There are so many people in our lives upon whom we can spread our blanket of warmth: a rebbi on his *talmidim*, parents on their children, and even children among each other. The warmth of this *ruck* never goes cold.

As all of these stories illustrate, the kindness we do for others takes on a life of its own, spreading goodness in the world and bringing goodness back into our own lives.

The Circle of Kindness

They say, "What goes around comes around." When you do an act of kindness, you create a merit of kindness in heaven. Then, when you face your own time of need, that merit may be waiting there, ready to help you. Thus, when you perform an act of kindness, you are not only helping another person, you are helping yourself as well.

In the early 1960's, air-conditioning was practically unknown in Eretz Yisrael. The summer heat permeated the houses, the buses, and streets, and there were few places to cool off and catch one's breath. Sandra Holtzer,* who was visiting from America, had taken on a mission that seemed simple at the outset. She just wanted to visit her son, but to do so, she had to make her way through the sweltering streets of Bnei Brak.

Mrs. Holtzer kept urging herself on, "A few more steps, a few more steps and you'll be there." As a survivor of the concentration camps, she had learned to will herself forward in the face of every kind of pain and exhaustion. "This is nothing," she chided herself. "You can do it."

Suddenly, a wave of vertigo overtook her. She felt as if the earth were tipping. Her knees buckled underneath her and she crumpled to the ground. There she lay, unconscious, as passersby flocked to the scene shouting, "Hatzolah! Hatzolah! A woman has fainted!"

A young man named Duvi was the first medic on the scene. He administered first aid and summoned an ambulance, which rushed Mrs. Holtzer to the hospital. Duvi sat by her side until she regained consciousness and then called her family members to alert them to the situation. Once he was certain that she was out of danger, he reassured her that she would be all right and left the hospital.

A few days later, Mrs. Holtzer was released from the hospital. She sought out Duvi right away to thank him for his kindness.

"Please, let me give you something," she said, handing him an envelope containing cash.

"I wouldn't think of it," Duvi replied. "I'm just glad I was able to help."

"Please," she said, "there must be something I can do for you."

"Well, I am getting married next week," Duvi told her. "I would be very grateful if you would come to my wedding and give my *kallah* a *berachah*."

Mrs. Holtzer gladly agreed to attend. "It's the least I could do," she added. "You really saved my life."

The night of the wedding arrived, and Mrs. Holtzer entered the wedding hall and headed toward the crowd that surrounded the *kallah*. At last, she made her way through the knot of well-wishers to introduce herself and offer her *berachah*. As she approached the young woman and looked at her face, a strange sense of familiarity washed over her. It was as if she were looking at an old friend, but how could that be?

"Mazal tov!" Mrs. Holtzer greeted the young woman. "I'm the lady your *chassan* rescued last week. Sandra Holtzer."

The *kallah* looked Mrs. Holtzer in the eye, and for a brief moment, neither of the women moved. Suddenly, the *kallah* shrieked. "Sandra! You said Sandra! Are you a survivor?"

Like a blurry picture snapping into focus, the *kallah's* face now emerged sharp and clear from Mrs. Hotzer's memory. "Saralah! Saralah, it's you!" she shouted, and within seconds, the two women were locked in a tearful embrace, weeping on each other's shoulders with abandon.

The crowd was perplexed. Who was this woman, and what was her relationship to the *kallah*? Soon the story emerged.

During the war years, Mrs. Holtzer endured the misery of the concentration camps with the help of a tight-knit group of friends who were interned along with her. In better days, they had attended Bais Yaakov together. They had committed themselves to living lives of dignity and devotion to Hashem. Nevertheless, they found themselves thrust into a world of inhumanity and cruelty, a world in which survival at any cost was the only relevant principle.

For this group of girls, however, the idea of sinking into a "survival of the fittest" mentality ran against every belief they held dear. They spoke to each other about the lowliness they saw all around them, and pledged that they would help one anther maintain their identities as daughters of Hashem, even in the "valley of death" that surrounded them. They picked up each other's spirits when despair reared its head. They reminded each other that salvation would come soon, and that when it came, they would emerge from their nightmare with their humanity and dignity intact.

One day, a transport of new arrivals came to the camp. Some of the new women were assigned to Mrs. Holtzer's barracks, and among them was a frightened young woman who was carrying a sack. Once she was certain that the prisoners were alone in the barracks, free from the watchful eyes of the guards, she opened her sack and carefully removed its unusual contents.

A gasp came forth from the other women. It was a child — a little girl!

The women's faces lit up with delight. How long had it been since they had seen a living child! Little Saralah brought a moment of pure, unadulterated happiness into their pain-numbed hearts. But almost immediately, their joy was overshadowed by the massive, looming question: How would they keep her fed, cared for, and undetected by the Nazis? There was no question that if she were discovered, she would be dead seconds later, along with whoever was accused of harboring her.

Nevertheless, there before Mrs. Holtzer's eyes was a Jewish child whose life was in danger. Despite the risks, she dedicated herself to keeping the girl safe. She hid the child in the barracks and fed her with small contributions solicited from the other, starving inmates. Against all odds, the arrangement worked out for several weeks. Saralah was the beloved child of the barracks, and the women were her doting mothers.

One day, Mrs. Holtzer heard news that sent a shock of fear through her heart. The Nazis had decided to clear out all the barracks and conduct a thorough search for contraband. The women were certain that Saralah was doomed.

But Mrs. Holtzer would not leave the little girl's fate to the Nazis. She decided to take a desperate measure; there was, after all, nothing more to lose. She packed little Saralah back into the sack in which she had arrived, and loaded the sack into the truck that collected the garbage. This was emptied into a dumpster located near the fence that separated the women's side of the camp from the men's. From there, Mrs. Holtzer took the precious sack and threw it over the fence. Once the Nazis had finished their search, she got a male prisoner to throw the sack back over to the women's side. Saralah was taken back to the barracks, and there she remained, safe and cared for, until the camp was liberated.

As the survivors began putting the shards of their lives back together after the war, Mrs. Holtzer lost track of Saralah. She had heard at one point that her camp "daughter" had settled in Israel, but they had, until this moment, never contacted each other. Now, as Mrs. Holtzer beheld precious Saralah, dressed in white and awaiting her journey into life as a Jewish wife and mother,

Hashem's *hashgachah* shined clear and strong. The child Mrs. Holtzer had helped to save was marrying the young man who had saved Mrs. Holtzer's life. The kindness had come full circle.

No act of kindness is ever forgotten in this world or the next.

A Blizzard of Warmth

The streets were piled with snow and the cars were stuck in their place. People were slipping and sliding as they tried to go on with life after the storm. As I walked the streets, I noticed the chesed that was being done all around. People were helping to push neighbors' cars out of the snow. Young men supported the elderly as they walked to shul. It then occurred to me that perhaps Hashem sometimes brings a snowstorm just to bring out acts of kindness in His children. In this story, Rabbi Benzion Klatzko tells us of such a chesed-generating storm.

Every year, I take a group of secular college students on a trip to Israel. They daven at the Kotel Friday night, visit Kever Rochel and experience a warm, traditional Shabbos in Yerushalayim. As they absorb a sense of what it means to live a Jewish life, they sometimes find themselves wanting more. Some even enroll in yeshivah and remain there for years. Experience has proven that this vehicle for *kiruv* is one with the power to carry a Jewish soul all the way from assimilation to a life of Torah and mitzvos.

Anticipating just such an inspiring trip, I arranged for a group of students to join me in Israel during their two-week winter break. I booked a flight for December 26, 2010, leaving from JFK, but Hashem had other plans for us.

On the days before our departure, I had been hearing reports of a major snowstorm of historic proportions, heading straight to the New York area. To be on the safe side, I left my home in Monsey 6 full hours before the scheduled 12:00 a.m. flight, leaving me several extra hours in which to contend with traffic slow-downs. As I pulled out of my driveway, the snow was already falling hard. On the highway, there were near white-out conditions. I crawled along, focusing on the lights of the car ahead of me like a sailor keeping watch on the North Star. What should have been an-hour-and-a-half trip from Monsey to JFK took 9 hours; it was 3 a.m. when I reached the airport.

The scene at the terminal was pure chaos. Aside from my group, there were a number of other groups leaving on Jewish outreach trips that evening, for a total of 220 students. The students were scheduled to depart in two shifts. One group, which was booked on the 6 p.m. flight, was stuck on the runway where EL AL kept them in a determined effort to take off as soon as the pilot received clearance. Finally, even EL AL had to concede that clearance was not coming any time soon. The passengers were allowed to disembark at 3 a.m. after 9 hours on the runway. The other half of the students were left waiting in the terminal.

Everyone was grumpy, hungry, tired and some were ready to forgo the entire trip. They were told that it might take two days before flights could resume. There was a sense of panic in the air.

I knew how important this trip to Israel was for these students, and I didn't want them to cancel. If they did, the likelihood of them signing up a second time was very slim. Those students would never have the chance to get that first wonderful taste of Judaism, and their holy souls might be lost to their people.

There was nothing for me to do but try to distract them while I thought of a better plan. For three hours, I told them stories and involved them in various games. By 6 a.m., the little bit of magic I had left was gone. Something had to happen, and fast. I decided to try to contact people in the nearby Five Towns area who I knew were involved and interested in *kiruv* and *chesed*. These were people who had signed up on my Shabbos hospitality website, shabbat.com, so at the very least, I knew they had their fellow Jews in their hearts.

Without any idea of what the response would be, I sent out a message that I had 220 Jewish students who were stranded at the airport and needed food, and perhaps a bed to rest in for a few hours. Nothing could have prepared me for what happened next. My cell phone began to buzz nonstop with calls from people who wanted to help. The offers were coming in faster than the snow was falling.

People began to arrive at the airport driving SUVs and vans full of food. Sixty pizza pies, heaps of bagels, pounds of fresh cream cheese and lox, dozens of donuts, hot coffee ... it was an amazing and welcome sight. I quickly solicited some volunteers and we set up shop. People were lining up and we were handing out pizza left and right. The smiles on my students' faces as they received such bounty, given with an open hand by people they didn't know, told me that this episode was having a strong impact on them

But it wasn't only my students who discovered the *chesed* in the heart of the Jewish people. The non-Jews, too, were recipients of our overflowing supplies. Passengers, flight staff, and security guards all got their empty stomachs filled courtesy of the Jews of the Five Towns. "You Jewish people are something special," I heard from more than one beaming face. "Blessed be your G-d!" another shouted out. It was one of the most magnificent moments of *kiddush Hashem* that I have ever seen.

Meanwhile, our rescuers were piling groups of students into their awaiting cars and taking them to homes in the area where they were able to shower and get some rest. Another group of students went to Yeshiva Shor Yoshuv in nearby Far Rockaway, where they were able to spend a few hours learning. It was truly an amazing sight.

Eventually the snow was cleared enough for us to continue on our trip. It was an outstanding one, which ended with many students deciding to stay on and learn in yeshivah. At the end of the trip, we conducted a survey and asked our students, among other questions, "What was the highlight of your trip?" Many of the students responded that the airport was the highlight. As one student explained, "It was the opportunity to see so much kindness done on our behalf. It was a real life example of a Torah community in action. And actions speak louder than words!"

In the end, it was clear that the snowstorm did not hinder our trip but actually led to its tremendous success. Local newspapers picked up the story and the *kiddush Hashem* was magnified tenfold. Through this unforgettable episode, I learned that Hashem sometimes brings what appears to be a storm in order to see His children unite to brave it. On that December day, the snow was melted by a radiant flood of warmth, which shone out from the heart of Klal Yisrael for everyone to see and remember.

There is nothing that surpasses the power of ahavas Yisrael to draw Jews — both those who are near and those who are far — closer to their people and their heritage.

Chapter 5:

Serving Hashem With All Your Heart

A Soldier's Battle

Torah and mitzvos have been the source of Klal Yisrael's strength and protection throughout the generations. And just as that is true on a national level, we must always realize that this is the source of our success on a personal level as well. In this story a man learns how to achieve victory.

"Stay around after davening," said Amram Kohen* to his friends in shul. "I'm making a *kiddush* today."

No one in the shul knew what Amram might be celebrating with this impromptu Shabbos *kiddush*. He hadn't mentioned any *simchah*. No baby, no bar mitzvah, no *aufruf*, no *siyum*. But the word went around to the *mispallelim* and when davening was over, they filed into a small room off to the side of their *shtiebel*, where the tables were arrayed with cakes, food, and drink.

Amram made *kiddush* on a cup of sweet red wine. He was obviously happy and at home with this group of Chassidishe men in this little *shtiebel* in the heart of Yerushalayim. His full beard, broad fur *shtreimel* and long, silk Shabbos *bekishe* gave him the look of a wise and benevolent king.

"So come on, Amram, tell us, what's the occasion?" one of his friends cajoled. "Are you planning to make a *kiddush* for us every week?"

Amram chuckled. "Well ... no. I've got to leave for a few minutes," he said mysteriously. "But if you stick around, you'll see why I made this *kiddush*." He walked out, leaving the men to play a guessing game as to what their friend had in store.

After 20 minutes had passed, the men were tiring of the wait. "I know what the surprise is," said one. "He's figured out how to get us all to stand here until Minchah!"

But Amram was no prankster. He was a beloved and well-respected member of the shul whose wholeheartedness shone through in his prayers. He loved everyone, but he loved his Gemara most of all. It was unlike him to waste anyone's time, and so the men held on for a few more minutes.

Their patience was rewarded when the door flung open, and in walked a soldier dressed in full uniform, helmet atop his head, holding the hand of a young boy. As the soldier came closer to the men, they realized that they were looking at the familiar face of their friend Amram. A stunned silence pervaded the room.

Amram surveyed the confused faces of his friends and broke into a warm smile. "So, you must all be wondering what happened to me, right? Why am I wearing a soldier's uniform to a *kiddush* on Shabbos? There's a story I want to share with you all, which will explain everything:

You all know me as Amram the Chassid, but it was not always that way. I am a *baal teshuvah* who grew up in a *chiloni* house, and led a very secular lifestyle. In fact from a young age I was taught to distrust the *chareidim*, and I always felt animosity toward anything or anyone religious.

But I had my ideals. And my highest ideal was to join the army and protect our land. As soon as I was old enough, I joined the army and worked as I hard as I could to advance my career. Over the years I progressed and gained higher and higher ranks until I became the commander of a very elite unit of 800 soldiers.

We were the very best of the Israeli Army. We were assigned the very dangerous missions that no one else could attempt, and we did whatever it took to protect our country. During this time, the Yom Kippur War took place. Without warning, the country was being attacked on all fronts and there had been no time to call up reserves or plan a response. My unit was summoned for an emergency meeting with the Prime Minister and Chief of Staff.

The situation was very bleak. We were told that we had to buy Israel enough time to make a proper counterattack. The only way to do so was to send our unit into the thick of the battle in the Golan to hold off the Syrians long enough to give us time to regroup.

They told us right then and there that our chances of survival were very slim. We could expect to lose 90 percent of our men. It was basically a suicide mission, but we were asked to make this sacrifice for the good of our country. When the general asked if we were ready for the task, we all shouted, "Yes!"

We gathered our equipment and headed out in jeeps toward the Golan. As I led our group, I realized that for most of us, this could be the final mission. But we did our best to come up with a reasonable battle strategy and hoped for the best.

When we arrived at the front, the air was thick with bullets and grenades. Somehow, we managed to surprise the enemy and push them back. It was a brutal battle, but when the smoke cleared, we had won. We had lost thirty men, which was of course thirty lives too many. However, in contrast to the hundreds we expected to lose, it was a miracle. As weary as we were, we were riding high on this astounding victory that defied logic. Best of all, we had succeeded in giving the defense forces the space they needed to call up the reserves and mount a counterattack. The rest, as they say, is history.

A few days after Succot, I decided that I would invite a rabbi to come and speak to our heroic unit. I had some important questions that needed to be answered. I approached one of the great Jerusalem rabbis and invited him to speak at our army base. He asked me if any of the soldiers were religious and I told him that they were not. He responded that there would be no point in him coming to speak in that case. But I pushed him, telling him that even non-religious soldiers would benefit from words of inspiration. Finally, he agreed to come.

When the rabbi arrived, we ushered him into a big hall where 800 seats were set up. On each of the thirty empty seats of the fallen soldiers, we had placed a large picture of the soldier in order to keep them all in mind and honor their memories. I stepped up to the podium and gave a rousing speech about the might of the Israeli Army.

Of course, I ascribed our entire victory to our high-level training and courage. Hashem did not enter into the picture at all.

I saw the disapproving look on the rabbi's face as I spoke, but that was nothing compared to the expression of shock that greeted my next comment.

Looking straight at the rabbi, I told my men, "I have brought a great rabbi from Jerusalem here today to answer a question that has been bothering me for some time now. I am sure it is a question that you all have as well. Here is my question, Rabbi.

"Everyone in this room was willing to give his life and soul for our country. We were all willing to die so that the country could live. We went on a suicide mission for our country, and were ready to do whatever it took to save our people.

"Dear Rabbi, where were the *chareidim*? They did nothing to help our country! We gave our blood and soul and the *chareidim* gave up nothing. Do you think that is right, Rabbi?"

The rabbi was a bit shaken by the question. He didn't know that I was setting him up, that I wasn't really calling on him to give us *chizuk*, but rather I was using him as a means by which to mock the *chareidim*.

The rabbi put his head down for a moment, appearing to be deep in thought. The soldiers watched and waited silently to hear how he would respond.

After a few moments, the rabbi lifted his head and looking out at the men, he replied, not with the consternation and guilt I had imagined I would induce, but with force and confidence: "Nothing? You think we did nothing? That is absolutely not true! I will tell you what we did. We davened our hearts out on Yom Kippur for you to succeed, so that Hashem would save us. Every *chareidi* cried out with heart and soul for Hashem to save us from our enemies.

"Do you know that the army contacted the chief rabbi and told him that they should be prepared to bury 70,000 men, because that was the expected onslaught? They were afraid there wouldn't be enough time to bury the dead, so they wanted us to prepare graves in advance!

"Then do you want to know what we did? A meeting was called of all the roshei yeshivah in Israel. At that meeting it was suggested that *bein hazmanim* this year should be cancelled. We needed the power of the Torah to protect our country and our soldiers more then ever. So the yeshivos remained open. While you battled on the fields, we battled in the *batei midrashim*. We didn't move from there. We learned and davened for you 24/7.

"Can you tell me there weren't any miracles performed for you? You yourself told me that that bombs that should have exploded near you didn't explode for some reason, and great tragedies were averted when their missiles missed their mark. And then somehow your impossible attack in the Golan succeeded miraculously. You hit your target each and every time. How? Was it not G-d Himself who was leading you into battle?

"We, my friends, were battling alongside you every step of the way. You fought with guns, we fought with prayer, and together we had the merit to win this war. Look around you. Does anyone here really believe that you won because of your own strength? Don't be foolish. There were clear and open miracles, and even a child could see that. So I ask you all to give this war and my words today a little thought, and I am sure you will all come to the same conclusion. We were partners in this war and that is why Hashem saved us all."

The soldiers, stirred by the rabbi's heartfelt words, burst into applause. My heart was stirred as well, and I had no reply to offer. The truth rings true, even to an unbelieving heart. Nevertheless, my mind was thrown into disarray. Could Torah and *tefillah* have really saved us?

Bursting with restless energy, I left the hall and started to jog. I ran and ran, working off the tension inside me. I ran past the gate of the base and onto the road. I ran along the road for miles, and I came to a yeshivah. There I stopped. Catching my breath, I walked deliberately inside the building and approached the first yeshivah student I saw.

"Let me ask you something," I said to him. "What were you doing during the war?

"I was learning Torah," the young man replied simply.

"But what about your yeshivah break? Don't you have off after Yom Kippur?"

"This year we couldn't take a break in our learning," he replied. "There was a war going on and our soldiers needed the protection of our Torah learning."

I was stunned by the straightforwardness of his answer. It was as if I had asked a soldier what he had been doing during the war and he replied, "fighting and shooting." What other answer could there be? Still, I had my doubts, so I resumed my run until I came upon another yeshivah. There, I asked the same question and I got the same answer.

It was at that moment that I realized that I had been wrong for many years, and that it was time for me to seek out the truth. I slowly but surely became a *chozer b'teshuvah*. Once I grasped the truth, I never let it go. I went to a yeshivah to learn Torah and then I got married and together with my wife, began building a Jewish home.

Today I am making a *kiddush* in honor of my youngest son, who is starting yeshivah. I want to show him that armies and soldiers alone cannot win wars. Torah and *tefillah* win wars. I want him to know that as he enters yeshivah, he is entering the most elite unit of the most elite army ever created.

It was a lesson his son and the entire shul would never forget.

In the Footsteps of Rav Gav

Rav Gavriel Klatzko was a born leader. Originally from Cleveland, Ohio, he learned for a few years in Israel and then, following his marriage, relocated his family to South Africa. There, he became the Rav of the Sunny Road Shul, a place where every Jew felt at home. It was during his tenure as Rav that his unique kiruv abilities and ahavas Yisrael became legendary. He brought hundreds, if not thousands, of people back to their Jewish heritage, until his life's work was cut short by his untimely death in 1999 at the age of 28. Although his years were short, his impact would last an eternity. In this story, Rabbi Benzion Klatzko tells us about the impact his younger brother made on him, and how he was inspired to walk in Rav Gav's footsteps, keeping his memory and his legacy alive.

I was not born a *kiruv* rabbi. I grew up in Cleveland, Ohio and learned in Telshe and the Mirrer Yeshivah. Nevertheless, even as a young man, I gained some leadership experience as part of my job leading *Pirchei* (Jewish youth) groups. After many years in that position, I naturally gravitated toward becoming a rabbi, and a few years after my marriage, I was asked to lead the Pirchei Agudas Yisrael Shul on 14th Ave in Boro Park.

Rabbi Gavriel Klatzko

I had been in that position for about six years when I became eager to accomplish more with my life. My job in Boro Park largely consisted of giving a *derashah* on Shabbos and a *shiur* during the week, but I wasn't changing lives. Therefore, when I was offered the chance to become a Rav in the community of Perth Amboy, New Jersey, I jumped at the opportunity. I felt that there, I would be able to make a real impact.

During my time in Perth Amboy, I learned how to be a jack of all trades. I had to become versed in the laws of building and maintaining an *eruv*, and in how to repair and maintain the local *mikveh*. I learned how to perform *bris milah* from Rabbi Benzion Krohn, and presided over weddings and funerals as well. I felt that I was making great headway in developing the community, and it was gratifying to see Jewish life there taking on a new vigor.

Then one Shabbos, my younger brother Gavriel came to Perth Amboy for a visit. He looked around at the shul and the community and he asked me "Is this it?"

"What do you mean, 'Is this it?' We have an *eruv* and a *mikveh* and everything a community needs," I replied incredulously. How could he have failed to notice what I had accomplished?

Truthfully, my brother knew me better than I knew myself at that time. While I was satisfied with my small *kehillah* and felt that I could have stayed there indefinitely, he knew that I could accomplish so much more.

It was not too long after that conversation that I got the phone call that turned my life upside down. My younger brother Gavriel had suddenly passed away, leaving behind a young wife and children, and hundreds of followers who were devastated by the loss of their Rav and leader.

My brother Gavriel was an exceptionally talented young man. He had been learning and working in *kiruv* at Ohr Somayach in Yerushalayim when, at the age of 26, he decided to pull back on his involvement in *kiruv* and devote more time to learning. The perfect situation soon presented itself — a *kollel* in South Africa was just starting up. Its members would be learning all day, and spending evenings reaching out to the community. Gavriel was accepted; he picked up his family and moved to South Africa.

Rabbi Benzion Klatzko teaching college students

Within 24 hours of his arrival, he was approached by representatives of a shul called the Sunny Road Synagogue. They needed a rav and wanted Gavriel. They made him a great offer, and he accepted.

During the two years in which he held that position, he managed to reach out to countless people, inspiring them, befriending them, and guiding them back to their Father in Heaven. When he died tragically in the middle of the night, his loss left them all bereft. I was of course heart-broken at my brother's *levayah,* but at the same time, I was awed and amazed by the crowd of more than a thousand people who had come to pay tribute to this young man. In just a few short years, he had touched the hearts and changed the lives of so many Jews.

But the *levayah* was just the beginning of my discovery of how my brother had lived his life. The *shivah* was a mind-boggling flood of stories from those who knew him.

One man said to me, "I had met your brother for 5 minutes and he had changed my life."

"What do you mean?" I asked

He said, "I was a *oleh chadash* living in Israel, and I was sitting on an Egged bus in Jerusalem. This young man gets on board and sits down next to me and greets me with a hearty *shalom aleichem*. I figured he must be from out of town or something, because he was so friendly. After a minute or two, he introduced himself. 'Hi, my name is Gavriel Klatzko, and I have an important question for you.'

"'Okay, what's your question?' I asked half-jokingly.

"'What are you doing for the Jewish people?'

"I said, 'Excuse me, what do you mean?'

"'Really I want to know. You seem like a very talented person. You are articulate, knowledgeable, and have a distinguished presence.We need people like you to help Klal Yisrael! Someone like you should be involved in reaching out to our lost brothers and sisters. You can have such a deep impact on our people! So what are you doing?'

"I didn't know what to answer. A few minutes later, your brother got off the bus at his stop and wished me well.

"That entire night, his question burned inside of me, and so the very next day I decided I had to do something. I enrolled in an Arachim class to learn how to teach Torah to non-religious people. Today I am one of the leading lecturers for Arachim and it is only because of my brief, but life-changing encounter with your brother."

That was my brother, always looking for ways to change the world, always seeking out Jews and trying to inspire them to bring out their best.

There is another amazing story that happened when Rabbi Mordechai Becher visited my brother in South Africa. They were walking together in a local park, in the midst of a deep discussion, when they noticed two Afrikaners who were obviously part of some gang.

My brother suggested to Rabbi Becher that perhaps one of the men was Jewish, and nobody would know, because everyone would be afraid to approach them. "Why don't we approach them?" he suggested.

Rabbi Becher thought it sounded like a very dangerous idea, with a very slim likelihood of a positive result. Neither of those objections deterred my brother, though. He fearlessly approached the two men.

"Hi, my name is Rav Gav," he said without hesitation. "Are either of you Jewish?"

The two men turned a deadly stare toward my smiling brother, but Gavriel didn't back down. Suddenly, one of them mumbled, "I am a little Jewish."

"Yeah, what do you mean?" my brother asked.

"Well, my mother's mother was Jewish," the man told him.

"Well, you know that means that you're Jewish, right?"

"Maybe it does technically, but I don't do anything Jewish."

"You don't do anything Jewish? You know, I never met anyone Jewish who didn't do anything Jewish. There must be something Jewish that you do."

"Well, I will tell you there is one thing. You see, ever since the *intifada* began and terrorists began to attack Jewish people in Israel, I began to have questions about Judaism and the Jewish people. So I found a website and I have been asking a rabbi my questions for several months now. He's been answering all of my difficult questions."

As soon as the Afrikaner said that, Rabbi Becher turned to him and said, "Is your name Douglas, by any chance?"

"Yeah, Rabbi, how did you know?"

"I am Rabbi Becher. I can't believe this, but I am the one who has been answering your questions for the last few months!"

So here you have a Jew that no one would reach out to. Only my brother saw the *Yiddishe* spark that no one else in the world could see under that rough, tough facade. When I started to hear these stories, I began to realize the enormous extent to which my brother changed people's lives. He brought them out of the darkness and into the light of Torah and mitzvos.

The entire time during the *shivah,* as rabbanim and *gedolim* came to visit, I began wondering, how could a person have had such a profound affect on so many lives?

Then I realized that my brother was only 28 years old when he passed away. A person that age thinks he has all the time in the world to hit his stride and find himself. What really struck a chord in me was the urgency with which Gavriel lived his life, feeling that each moment was an opportunity that could not be wasted.

I was already two years older than Gavriel was when his life came to a halt. I realized that, in a blink of an eye, ten years would pass and I would still be in Perth Amboy doing my job as rabbi. Upon how many people would I be able to have an impact? Was I living with a sense of urgency, and if I wasn't, then how would I do my share in bringing the *Geulah*?

I began to think, "Who will fill Rav Gav's shoes if not me?" But what could I do?

Shortly after I finished *shivah* and went back to my home in New Jersey, a position opened up in California to do *kiruv* on the campus of UCLA. I saw this as the opportunity of a lifetime. It was as if Hashem were guiding me toward the fulfillment of my new dream — to reach out to college youth who hardly had any idea that they were Jewish, and bring them back to their spiritual home. I tried out for the job, and even though I had no experience, they saw the passion in my heart and they gave me my big chance.

Once I had settled into the campus, I developed a simple, straightforward way of meeting people. I would set up a little booth on the walkway, and as people walked by, I would ask them "Hi. Are you Jewish?"

Over the years, this approach has succeeded in helping me find and eventually influence Jews to connect with their heritage.

Someone once asked me how I could ask such a blunt question to total strangers without feeling embarrassed.

"Here's how I see it," I explained. "If these students who are walking by were actually walking onto a cattle-car, headed toward their deaths, I would have no problem trying to stop them from proceeding. Well, they are headed toward their spiritual death, and if I don't stop them then they will walk right into the spiritual gas chamber of assimilation and they will be lost to Klal Yisrael forever. They will intermarry and their offspring will not be Jewish. Embarrassment has no place in such a situation."

And thus, with the help of Hashem, I began to save many lives.

I believe that all of us have to live our lives with a sense of urgency and grab whatever opportunity comes our way to affect others for the better. We have a responsibility to live each day Hashem gives us in this world to its fullest, and make our Father in heaven proud. I learned from my brother to inspire others to the best of my abilities, and we can all learn from him to strive to reach our potential, in whatever area it lies.

Today I head a college campus *kiruv* program that has a potential impact on more than 100,000 lives each year. In my home in Monsey, I have the privilege of hosting 50 to 100 Jewish students each week, giving them a taste of what Shabbos can be.

As an outgrowth of my *kiruv* work, I launched a website called shabbat.com, where any Jew from anywhere around the globe can locate a place to eat and stay for Shabbos. More than 5,000 people each week are hosted through this website, and it is growing each day. The website also benefits the hosts, giving them the opportunity to reach out to their fellow Jews, and to teach their children that even today, we can be like Avraham Avinu, drawing people toward Hashem and creating new Jewish homes.

I believe that each and every one of us has the ability to make a lasting impact on others if we put our hearts to it. If we walk in the footsteps of Rav Gav, loving every Jew and guiding them back to their spiritual home, then with the help of Hashem, we will be able to count ourselves among those who are helping to hasten the coming of Mashiach, may it be soon and in our day.

If we want to live our lives in a way that makes a difference in the world, we must each ask ourselves Rav Gav's question: "What are you doing for the Jewish people?"

From the Depths of My Heart

Sometimes we go through difficult periods in life in which we feel that we are all alone. But we must never forget that we are never alone. It is precisely at that moment that we must hold onto Hashem with all our might and call out Shema Yisrael, and in that merit, Hashem will pull us out of the depths of darkness.

For Reb Avraham Frankel,* there were only two choices. He could begin his life anew, or he could struggle under the impossible burden of the misery he had endured during the war. The physical pain, the human cruelty and suffering, the complete subjugation of Hashem's holy people to a nation that had lost all sense of morality — once a person had experienced all that, how could he go on with life?

But then again, how could he *not* go on with life? How could he take the miracle of his survival and drown it in an endless pool of grief and confusion? The only thing that made sense was to tamp down the ghastly images and memories, place a tight lid on the entire episode and try to live again. And so, Avraham Frankel turned his whole heart to serving Hashem and raising a Torah-observant family.

He was determined that his children would have a carefree, innocent childhood, unhindered by frightening stories of the war. The children knew their father was a survivor, but they also knew that he did not wish to speak about his experiences. They grew up blessedly happy and healthy, and yet, there was one constant reminder of the unnamed terrors Reb Avrohom had endured: the fact that there was not one hair on either of his arms. The family knew that this was a result of some horrific episode, but the specific story was never revealed to them.

The years rolled forward and the children grew up to establish families of their own. The oldest grandchild, named Simcha, felt a special bond with his grandfather. In their moments together throughout the years, Simcha had often noticed his grandfather's unusual arms, and had several times begged for an explanation. Reb Avraham's response was always, "You're too young for such stories. Maybe at your bar mitzvah I will speak about it."

At last, the time of Simcha's bar mitzvah arrived. Simcha did not forget his grandfather's words.

"*Zeide*, tonight is my bar mitzvah," he reminded Reb Avraham. "You are going to tell us your story, right?"

"Yes, Simcha, a deal is a deal," Reb Avraham confirmed. "Tonight is the night."

The bar mitzvah began and the guests arrived at the hall. Simcha was the perfect guest of honor, graciously greeting the nonstop stream of well-wishers who sought him out to shake his hand, give him a hug, and slip a gift envelope into his hands. He was filled with delight, and yet, one thought occupied the corner of his mind. He periodically wove through the crowd to find his grandfather. "*Zeide*, when will you tell your story?" he asked. After all these years of restraining his curiosity, he could barely contain it for another minute.

"Not yet, Simcha. I am waiting for someone to come," Reb Avraham explained. "I can't tell the story until he is here."

Now Simcha's curiosity leapt to a new level. Who was the mystery guest? What did he have to do with *zeide's* story? All of these questions tumbled about inside his head, even as he recited his own speech flawlessly and whirled around the dance floor with his classmates and relatives.

The dancing stopped and the desserts were being carried out from the kitchen — two sure signs that the occasion was nearly finished. Simcha's heart was sinking. When would *zeide* tell his story? Soon, the guests would be gone and the moment would be lost.

Reb Avraham realized that he could not wait any longer for his special guest to arrive. Still scanning the room for some familiar face, he walked up to the lectern and asked the guests for a few moments of attention. Suddenly, the door opened and an elderly Jew walked in. The old man looked very sickly; he was bald and had no facial hair or *peyos* at all. When Reb Avrohom saw the old man, his face lit up. He abandoned the lectern to greet the man with a heartfelt hug, and then brought him by the hand to the head table, to sit by his side.

Then Reb Avraham began to tell his story — a story that had given him strength and inspiration throughout his life:

I grew up in a little *shtetl* in Poland. When the Nazis invaded, they rounded us up and loaded my entire family onto cattle-cars bound for Auschwitz. When we got there, the doors opened for the first time in days and we were forced off the trains into a scene I can never forget. We were greeted by soldiers with guns and barking dogs. Many had died on the train, and all of us who remained were weak and terror-stricken. I felt as if I had stumbled into a nightmare.

The Nazis lined us up in order to push us through the separation process, presided over by the infamous Dr. Mengele. With a flick of his finger, he sent most of the men and older boys to the right, where they were destined for slave labor, and most of the women and children to the left, to be marched off to their deaths. As I stood with the men on the right, a scene unfolded that would be forever seared into my memory.

I stood next to a boy named Shmuel, who was about my age – 15. He, along with his father and brother, had been separated from his mother and sisters. Shmuel's mother stood there, across from her son, looking at him with such longing. At last, she couldn't take it anymore and she dashed to her son's side and wrapped him in a motherly hug. A Nazi ran up right behind her, pulled her away and threw her to the ground. With no more thought than a person would employ to swat a fly, the Nazi pumped a bullet into this poor Jewish mother, leaving her dead on the ground.

Her daughters, now left alone on the women's side, shrieked in horror and ran to their mother. Two more gunshots went off and Shmuel's sisters were lying dead atop his mother. Shmuel's father could no longer stand there and helplessly watch his family being massacred. He threw himself at the Nazi, pummeling him with his fists, pouring out the last of his strength in a tragic effort to avenge his family's blood. Shmuel's brother joined in the fray, and within moments, they too were taken from this world.

There stood Shmuel. In less than 5 minutes, he had seen his entire family — his parents, sisters and brother — all slaughtered before his eyes. Hatred and vengeance burned in his eyes. His muscles were tensed for action, but he stood in his spot. His heart became an abyss, a bottomless pit of pain that he had no way of salving.

That was our introduction to Auschwitz. The next activity the Nazis had prepared for us was to cleanse us of the filth that, in their eyes, we Jews carried on our very beings. The only way to get rid of such filth was to burn it off, and so, they marched us out to a pit filled with water and lye. We were ordered to jump in, one by one, quickly immerse our heads and then jump out. There was no problem getting us to emerge quickly, for more than a moment or two in that solution would produce painful burns.

Down the line, the boys each took their turn in the bath. Then Shmuel's turn arrived. He refused to budge from his place. We boys, who had witnessed the shootings of his family at the selection site, could not bear to see the one survivor shot dead. "Do it, Shmuel," we urged. "It's not so bad. At least you'll live!"

Finally, without a word, he jumped in, but he would not immerse his head. The Nazi in charge of us pointed a gun at him and ordered him to duck under water. After a brief delay, he did what he was told to do, but then a few moments passed and he had still not resurfaced. The tension among the boys shot up to a new level of desperation. If he stayed submerged for another few moments, that would be it; he would die a horrible death. To the Nazi, it would mean nothing, but the boys could not bear the thought.

Suddenly, one of the boys leaned over the pit and immersed his arms in the lye solution and groped blindly for Shmuel. He felt Shmuel's shoulders, wrapped his hands underneath them and pulled with all his might. Scorched from head to toe and shrieking in pain, Shmuel emerged alive. His rescuer's arms were also severely burned; there was not a hair left on them.

When Shmuel had recovered some of his composure, I asked him why he had stayed submerged in the deadly pool.

"When I went underneath the water, I had a silent conversation with Hashem. I told Him, 'I have lost everything — my parents, my brother and sisters, my home. I have absolutely nothing left in the world besides You. That is the one thing I will never let the Nazis take away from me. I am going to die in this hole while my *neshamah* screams *Hashem echad u'shemo echad* (Hashem is one and His Name is one).'

"When I felt you pulling me out of the pool, I thought it was Hashem's hands pulling me out. I didn't even realize it was human hands. I was in middle of shouting *Shema Yisrael* in my head."

Rabbosai, I was that boy who stuck his hands into the lye to save Shmuel and that is the reason that I don't have any hair on my arms. It never grew back again. And I want you to know that this man sitting up front with me tonight at the head table is my dear friend Shmuel — a man from whom we could learn so much.

My dear grandson, my message to you tonight is as follows: You may know *tzaddikim* and you may have pictures of great *gedolim* hanging on your wall. But this man sitting at the head table who doesn't have hair on his face or body, he knows the meaning of *Hashem echad u'shemo echad*. The biggest *berachah* I could give you in life, my dear grandson, is to know that no matter what situation you are in, Hashem is always there for you. If you ever find yourself in deep trouble and don't know what to do, remember, *Hashem echad u'shemo echad.*

No matter what a person loses in his life, he is not lost, as long as he maintains his connection, deep in his heart, to the One and Only Hashem.

With All Your Soul

Rabbi Tzvi Hirsch Meisels was known as the Veitzener Rav. He was a leader before the war and a hero to his people during the war while imprisoned in the concentration camps. The Jews knew they could count on him for advice and encouragement, and that he would risk his life to help them to perform mitzvos in the most difficult situations. After the war, he was appointed as Rav of Bergen-Belsen. Eventually he moved to America and established a thriving kehillah in Chicago. The following story, which Rabbi Meisels recounted in his sefer, "Mekadshei Hashem," tells of mesirus nefesh for a mitzvah and of kiddush Hashem.

Before the war, I owned a *tallis,* which I had received from my father-in-law, the Rav of Limanov. This *tallis* bore an *atarah* (an ornamental neckpiece attached to the *tallis)* that had belonged to the Sigheter Rav. The day that I was deported to

Auschwitz, I managed to take this precious *tallis* along with me, believing that as long as I could wrap myself within its holy confines, the Nazis and their horrors could not penetrate.

That sense of protection, along with everything else I owned, was snatched away from me as soon as I arrived at Auschwitz. There, the Nazis immediately confiscated all personal possessions, and my *tallis* was thrown upon the heap of other cherished belongings that people had chosen to accompany them into this nightmare.

Without my *tallis,* I felt terribly vulnerable, a knight without his spiritual armor. I was determined to locate it as soon as I possibly could, and to that end, I managed to get myself assigned to the task of sorting through the confiscated clothing and valuables to be packed up and shipped to Germany. One day, while doing my job, I chanced upon my lost *tallis*. My heart filled with joy, and with great difficulty, I smuggled it back to the barracks.

Now that I had the *tallis,* I realized that putting it on under the watchful eyes of the kapos would be too big a risk. But my longing for this mitzvah was so very great that I took a desperate measure — I cut the *tallis* down into a pair of *tzitzis* which, if I was careful and discrete, I could wear under my prisoner's uniform. To my great delight, I managed to wear the *tzitzis* in a way that did not create a telltale bulge, and I wore them every day.

One day as I was leaving the bathhouse, the chief of the kapos, a man named Foenix, yelled for me to halt. Foenix was a German communist who was serving a life sentence for his crimes. One of his tasks was to ensure that no prisoner dressed in more than one layer of clothing. When he noticed a slight bulge in my uniform, he quickly surmised and that I was wearing something under my uniform.

"What is this?" he shouted at me while yanking at the *beged*.

I did not want him to think that I had stolen the garment, so I said, *"Es ist ein Gotteskleid"* — it's a religious garment that I brought from home.

He immediately began to pound my head and body with heavy blows, accompanied by a barrage of curses.

"Come with me to my room," he commanded. "There I will teach you a few things about G-d!"

Everyone knew that such an invitation was bound to signal one's last moments on earth. Yet I had no choice but to follow him to his room, where, as expected, he began to beat me into unconsciousness. But his anger was motivated by something other than animal aggression. He had a theological agenda, which he screamed into my face as he went about his beating.

"Swine! You still speak of *Gotteskleid* at a time when you see with your own eyes, daily, the obliteration of your family and your nation, with every type of cruel and unnatural death imaginable. Under such conditions, you are still able to mention the Name of G-d and believe in Him and His control of the world? Why doesn't He stop the Nazis from exterminating your people? They suffer tortures the likes of which no son of man has ever been made to bear. This I know is sure: There is no judge and there is no justice in this world!"

I was lying on the ground like an inanimate stone, deep in pain and falling rapidly into despair. I lay there, unwilling to move, until the kapo commanded me to stand up and answer his tirade. I knew he would not hesitate to kill me if he was dissatisfied with my answer.

"Let me explain it to you with a parable," I said with every shred of strength I could call upon. "A renowned surgeon was called in to operate on a gravely ill, high-ranking officer. In order to remove a life-threatening obstruction, he had to cut out large chunks of the diseased tissue. Now, if a simple shoemaker were to watch the surgery, he would be horrified. 'This butcher is cutting up the poor officer for no good reason. When I cut up shoes I certainly don't cut up the beautiful soft top leather.'

"I ask you, Foenix, do you think that the surgeon would change this necessary procedure because of the criticism from the ignorant shoemaker? No! He would take all the steps that are necessary to save the patient's life.

"The same could be said about G-d. We don't understand His ways. We cannot fathom why he cuts up the noblest part of the Jewish people. Yet we must realize that the fact that we mere humans can't fathom His ways does not take away from His supremacy."

I concluded with an insight that I had heard from my father. The reason the Rav of Yaroslav lived a long life was because he never questioned G-d's ways. He accepted any adversity he encountered with love. He used to say, "I am afraid that G-d will say, 'If you question My ways, you can come up to heaven and there, you will see that everything is done with justice and fairness.' Since I had no desire to go up to heaven prematurely, I never questioned G-d's ways."

"I want to give you some advice, Foenix," I said to the silent kapo. "Don't ask questions about the way G-d is handling the affairs of the world. I know that you, too, are hoping to be set free one day and to start a new life. So I suggest that you not challenge G-d's ways unless you would like to join Him sooner than expected."

Thank G-d, my words impressed him.

"You are a smart Jew," he said with a smile. "I will let you go. And from now on you can come to my barracks and pick up a good meal." Foenix allowed me to keep my precious *tzitzis* and spared my life.

That was how Hashem saved me from certain death on that day. For this I give thanks to Hashem, for, as *Tehllim* declares, "He is good and His kindness endures forever."

Eventually, I was transferred to a labor camp that held 1,500 Jewish prisoners. A few weeks before our liberation by the American forces, the Germans evacuated the camp, and began to move us around to prevent us from being set free by the Americans. On the Shabbos before our liberation, we could clearly hear the explosions of American artillery shells falling. We realized that the Americans were approaching our camp, and liberation was at hand. But would we live to see the day?

Suddenly, an order was given for us to line up to be shipped to another location. We suspected that this was the final chapter; they would finish us off before the Americans could find us.

Whenever we were shipped to a new camp, the kapos would search the prisoners for items to steal; they had no qualms about taking our shoes, clothes, or any hidden valuables we had managed to keep. Hoping to strike it lucky, Willy, the kapo in charge of our barracks, frisked every inmate. When he got to me, he found my pair of *tzitis*. In his disappointment over the meagerness of his find, he ripped them off of me and threw them into a burning stove.

I couldn't believe it. After all this time, all that I had been through with these *tzitzis* as my protection, they were gone up in smoke. Here we were, about to embark on what may well have been our last journey in life, and I was left defenseless. It was just too much to bear, and I broke down in a fit of hysterical weeping. My son Zalman Leib, who had been by my side throughout the war, tried to put me at ease.

"Look, Father," he said, "none of the 1,500 Jews here have worn a pair of *tzitzis* since the day they arrived in Auschwitz. Why be upset? Hashem, Who has helped us until now, will spread His wings over us and continue to protect us. He will release us from our distress in a short time!"

We were marched to a railroad platform and loaded into cattle-cars. We stood in the stifling heat, pressed up against each other without food or drink. We were hoping that the Americans would arrive before the Germans had the chance to harm us.

Sleep was the only thing that brought relief, and the only way to sleep was by resting our heads on the shoulder of the person next to us. I rested my head on my son's shoulder and I was able to doze off. Willy the kapo was sleeping soundly, stretched out on a wooden bench he had placed in the middle of the cattle-car.

Before long, my son woke me up. "Tatte," he moaned. "My shoulder hurts so badly, I can't take the pain. Could you please rest your head on another person's shoulder?" For a moment, I was upset at being awakened, but I quickly changed my position and leaned my head on the other fellow's shoulder.

Suddenly, we were surrounded by a deafening sound. Bombs came crashing down all around us. The American bombers obviously thought they were hitting a German troop transport. A piece of shrapnel came hurtling between Zalman Leib's shoulder and myself, precisely where I had been resting my head seconds earlier. Following its deadly course, the shrapnel continued its flight and struck Willy on the bench, slicing off both of his hands. Howling in pain, he begged for help. The people couldn't feel sorry for him

The author with Rabbi Zalman Leib Meisels

after the way he had mistreated us and had ruthlessly taken my *tzitzis* and thrown them into the fire. They jeered at him, "Now you don't have hands to harm us anymore, Willy"

"Please, please help me! Save me!" He screamed and wailed, "Rabbi, please forgive me! Pray for me that G-d should spare my life!"

In His mysterious way, Hashem sends pain and turns it into the instrument of blessing. And so, my annoyance of being stirred by my son from the peaceful escape of slumber turned out to be the blessing that saved my life. I had fallen asleep on my son's shoulder many, many times before, and never did he complain, yet this time, for some reason, the weight of my head caused unbearable pain that literally forced him to disturb my sleep. It was obvious that the Guardian of Israel, Who never slumbers or sleeps, was protecting me.

Everyone in that cattle-car realized that Hashem had protected me. They saw with their own eyes how Hashem had punished Willy for burning my *tallis*. With those two visions of Divine justice before their eyes, they were now confident that Hashem would help us survive the war as well.

We were left on the train without food or drink. To soothe the torment of hunger, we ate the grass and herbs that we gathered in the fields. I could not help but think of Adam's curse: *[The earth] will bring forth thorns and thistles for you, and you will eat the grass of the field (Bereishos 3:18).* For the first time in my life, I realized the nutritional value of what freely grew from the earth; it was enough to still our hunger somewhat, keeping us alive until we could obtain more substantial food.

It was Wednesday afternoon when we saw the German guards running away, leaving us free to roam. No doubt, the American forces were nearby. Within an hour the first American tank rolled into the camp, and pandemonium broke loose. We embraced and cried on each other's shoulders. Cheering loudly, the men lifted me high and carried me on their shoulders.

"Rabbi, you were the one to help us survive! It was your encouragement and *Tehillim* in the worst of times that opened wide the gates of heaven and awakened Hashem's mercy," they proclaimed.

Turning to the jubilant crowd I said, "*Rabbosai*, let us all say *Shema Yisrael* with fervor and *kavanah*. Let us accept wholeheartedly Hashem's sovereignty. Until today, we were standing at the threshold of death. We were in no condition to accept G-d's rule. But now that we have been liberated by the grace of G-d, we can accept His sovereignty with total dedication.

"Remember the verse, *All my limbs will say, Hashem, who is like You?* (*Tehillim* 35:10). These are the words that apply to the present moment, for we find that all of our limbs are intact after all of the beatings and the torment we suffered. We must recognize the hand of G-d, Who saved us from all of our enemies. Loudly we proclaim, 'All my limbs will say, Hashem, who is like You?'"

After the liberation, we learned that we had been saved from certain death. The reason the Germans moved us from place to place was because they were unable to carry out their plan of bringing us to a death camp for extermination. The railroad tracks were uprooted, and the bridges were destroyed. Hashem had foiled their plans so that He could grant us life and joy.

The mesirus nefesh of Rabbi Meisels to perform a mitzvah was not confined to tzitzis alone. Here is another story told about his courageous effort to find a way to immerse himself in a mikveh, right in the middle of Auschwitz.

In a place filled with death and defilement, Rabbi Meisels began to long for the opportunity to purify himself in a *mikveh*. Nevertheless, he realized that finding a *mikveh* in Auschwitz would be about as likely as finding a snowball in Gehinnom. Thus, his longing remained a longing, not an actual plan.

Then one day, Rabbi Meisels noticed that the camp had a large pit filled with water. Its purpose was to embellish the façade of humanitarianism that the Germans showed to the Red Cross on their infrequent inspections. The water was apparently a safety measure for use in case of fire — an ironic touch in a place where humans were routinely cremated.

But when Rabbi Meisels caught sight of this pit of water, he immediately began to dream of using it as a *mikveh*. His only concern was that the water seemed dangerously deep, and he doubted his ability, in his weakened state, to keep himself afloat.

The problem was solved by accident when Rabbi Meisels, walking back to his barracks from his work detail, passed the pit while a Nazi stood nearby, taunting a Jewish man. Without any warning, the Nazi lifted up the prisoner and tossed him into the pit. The man began screaming, "Help! I can't swim!"

Without a second thought, Rabbi Meisels jumped into the water and swam to the drowning man. The Nazi could easily have picked them both off in the water with a couple of bullets, but he preferred instead to watch the show. Rabbi Meisels managed to get the man out of the water, and in the process, he learned that it was not as deep as it looked. He decided that as soon as the opportunity presented itself, he would immerse.

A few nights later, Rabbi Meisels crept out of his barracks and found his way in the dark to the water pit. Joyfully, he immersed in the water, feeling the putrid residue of camp life washing away, leaving his soul shining and pure. He managed to repeat this revitalizing experience for several nights without any hindrance.

Then one night, as he was about to immerse, a guard spotted him. "Stop!" the guard ordered. "What are you doing here?"

Rabbi Meisels had a story prepared for the occasion. "I work in the kitchen and I just want to make sure that I'm clean so that when I handle the food, I won't get people sick," he claimed.

"Go ahead," said the Nazi. "Jump in and let me see you swim."

Unsure of what the Nazi was planning to do next, Rabbi Meisels jumped in and began swimming.

"Move!" shouted the Nazi. He threw a rock at the rabbi, who picked up speed in an effort to avoid being hit. More rocks showered down on him as he swam madly about, trying to avoid being knocked unconscious in the water. Eventually, the game grew tiresome for the guard and he ordered the rabbi out of the water. He never returned to the "*mikveh,*" but he was proud that he had been able to uphold this mitzvah and create a little purity, even in the depths of Auschwitz. Certainly, it was an accomplishment no one else could claim.

The incident illustrated Rabbi Meisel's determination to keep every mitzvah alive. This courage, which got him through the war, continued to serve him afterward as he led a *kehillah* and re-established Torah life in the post-war world.

I am reminded of a story I heard recently from Rabbi Fishel Schachter.

Reb Shmuel Benisch was a member of my shul who had survived the concentration camp. He would often tell us stories about his experiences, and this one taught me an especially vivid lesson.

At the end of the war, the Nazis took the remaining Jews on a death march. The irony for the prisoners was particularly bitter, because they knew that liberation was around the corner, and yet in their hunger and weakness, they fell by the hundreds as they struggled to keep moving along.

Those who made it to the end-point found themselves herded into a barn. Reb Shmuel felt that this might just be his last day on earth. He felt a great urge to daven Maariv and say the *Shema*, but the barn was filled with a foul odor. Therefore, he went outside and began to daven. A Jewish kapo saw him and asked him what he was doing.

"I want to daven Maariv but I can't do it inside because of the smell," he explained simply. The kapo nodded his assent and Shmuel began to pray. Meanwhile, the other kapos drifted over to the place in which he stood and laughed at the futility of his prayers. They began a song, whose bone-chilling lyrics were, "In the morning they will burn him alive, and tonight he davens Maariv."

They continued singing and laughing at Shmuel until their miserable spirit began seeping into his heart. He tried to concentrate, but the morbid lyrics broke through his concentration and threw his mind off track. He was about to quit when he stopped himself short. "Shmuel, do you hear what they are saying? Tomorrow they will burn you. That means that today might be your only opportunity to daven to Hashem. So do what you can today, and whatever happens tomorrow will happen!"

The more the kapos sang their death song, the more he prayed. He began dancing and singing and pouring his heart out to his Creator. At that moment, he felt he had won the battle with the kapos and with his own *yetzer hara.* No matter what tomorrow would bring, he had that victory.

A few hours later, he was back in the barn with the other prisoners, waiting for what seemed like certain death. Suddenly, loud gunshots could be heard outside the barn. Shmuel and the others pushed their way to the outside and saw the kapos lying dead on the ground, bullet wounds riddling their bodies. The Russians were coming from one side and the British from the other. Apparently, the fleeing Nazis saw that their end was near and wanted to ensure that the kapos, who knew well their monstrous crimes, would not be alive to testify against them. Shmuel looked at the bodies of the men who had sung of his imminent death and saw that it was they who would not see another day. For Shmuel, there would be a whole new beginning.

Rabbi Schachter concluded: Shmuel once said, "Do you know how many tomorrows I have gone through in my life in the last 50 years? I've had many ups and downs, and every time I was about to give up, I got a hold of myself and said, 'Shmuel, how many tomorrows have passed since that day? Imagine if you wouldn't have davened Maariv that night and would have listened to those kapos. Would you ever have forgiven yourself? Are you going to start worrying about tomorrow now? No, today you daven and then tomorrow, you will see that everything will work out.'"

When our worries about the future weigh us down, we must stop and look at the evidence. We're here today, alive and well, with food to eat and a place to live. Hashem hasn't let us down yet, so why not trust that He will take care of us tomorrow as well?

A Moo-ving Bris

The Gemara (Shabbos 130a) states that any mitzvah that Jews risk their lives to perform during a time of governmental persecution will remain forever rooted in our people. This applies to such situations as when bris milah is forbidden or idol worship is demanded at risk of death. Although today in America, such sacrifices seem to belong to a faraway times and places, it was not long ago that the Jews living in Communist Russia were indeed called upon to risk their lives to practice their faith. In this story, we meet one such hero.

A sense of happy expectation charged the atmosphere of the small shul. The father of the newborn boy and the *mohel* rushed around with a sense of purpose, while a small knot of men at the front of the shul grew gradually into a crowd. The women stood near the back of the room, positioning themselves to see and hear as much as possible. At last, a tiny infant borne on a pure white satin pillow appeared at the doorway, safely held aloft in the steady hands of a young woman.

"*Kvatter*!" called the *mohel,* and the *bris milah* ceremony was underway. The woman advanced through the room and handed her precious charge to her husband, who carried the baby to the front of the shul where the infant's father waited. Gently, the father set his son down on the *sandek's* lap, and after a few minutes of tense anticipation, the baby's cry was heard. His name was announced and blessings were showered upon him. He had been entered into the covenant of Avraham; he was a member of the tribe, a kosher Jewish boy.

It was far from an unusual occasion in this small shul in Queens, New York. With many young couples living in the community, dozens of families each year celebrated a son's *bris.* For the community, it was always a joyful occasion; for the parents, it was unforgettable and emotional. There is nothing quite like hearing the child's name called out for the first time, knowing that this is the name by which he will be called up for an *aliyah* at his bar mitzvah, and this is the name that will appear on his *kesubah.* This is the name under which his lifetime of mitzvos and *maasim tovim* will be inscribed.

With all the emotion attached to the occasion, the guests at the *bris* did not at first notice the tears being shed by the elderly Russian man, a newcomer to the neighborhood who gave his name as Igor. As the crowd began to head toward the festive meal that awaited them, Igor wove his way to the *mohel* and cried out, "Rabbi! Thank you!"

Tearfully, he embraced the *mohel* and repeated again and again, "Thank you, thank you." He continued on with a river of emotion-drenched words, all in Russian. The *mohel* tried to comfort Igor, but in truth, he had no idea what had sparked the torrent of tears.

The shul's rabbi, noticing the unusual scene, approached a congregant who spoke Russian and asked him to find out what was upsetting Igor. The two men conversed, and within a few minutes,

Igor had regained his composure. He had a story to tell, and with the help of the translator, he told it:

I grew up in a small Russian town as a part of a close-knit Jewish community. Although religion was officially forbidden, in our town the authorities were willing to look the other way. Therefore, we were able to daven in shul on Shabbos, to perform *bris milah,* and to have a kosher *chuppah* for our young people. We knew enough to keep our activities quiet, but we had enough freedom to lead some sort of proper Jewish life.

But when I was 14, all that changed. That was when the town was taken over by the Jewish Communists. They were bent on putting an end to our ways, which they saw as backward and superstitious. They were going to take us kicking and screaming into the modern world. In fact, they were so "civilized" that they declared that if anyone was discovered to have performed a *bris,* then the mother and the baby would be hung together in the town square.

This was a terrible decree for us, because we were not willing to compromise on *bris milah*. On the other hand, how could we perform a *bris* if it meant putting lives in danger? We had to devise some sort of strategy so that Jewish life could continue.

When the next boy in the community was born, we decided on a plan. We gathered together in the barn on our farm. My job was to hold a whip in my hand and every time the baby cried, I was to whip the cow hard so that it would moan aloud, and would thus obscure the baby's cries.

As soon as the *mohel* began to perform the *milah*, I began to whip the cow as hard as I could, and it began screaming out in pain. For me, it was a situation that was nearly impossible to bear. Here we were, performing such a sacred act in a barn, and here I was, inflicting pain on this senseless creature.

As I whipped the cow, I prayed to Hashem, "Please let me merit to attend a *bris* in a regular shul where I am not forced to hide behind animals to do Your mitzvos." I always longed for the day when I would be part of a regular *bris* in a shul again. Today was the first time in over 40 years that I was able to attend a *bris*. Finally, I have lived to see the day when I no longer have to perform this mitzvah in hiding. Today, my prayer has been answered.

Although we are not called upon to take such risks to perform a mitzvah, we are called upon to give of ourselves with the time, expense, and effort Hashem's mitzvos require. To the extent that we sincerely embrace these opportunities to perform Hashem's will, we will secure the love of Hashem's mitzvos for our future generations.

A Message From Above

Often, what we perceive as annoyances, irritations, or obstacles in our lives are, in fact, messages from Hashem. By allowing a little discomfort to come our way, He prods us to correct our course. Ultimately, if we heed these messages, we find that our challenges pave the way to our personal greatness.

Recently, I had the opportunity to take part in an *oneg Shabbos* that was organized in my neighborhood for a group of *baalei teshuvah*. In the midst of the singing, eating, and *divrei Torah*, one of the young men stood up and asked to speak. "I want to share with you what inspired me to become a religious Jew, because I think everyone here could learn from this experience," he told the group. Already reveling in the spirit of a beautiful Shabbos, the audience was eager to listen to his tale:

At the point in time when this story happened, I was still just dabbling in learning. Officially, I was enrolled in Aish HaTorah in the Old City, but I found it difficult to spend more than a few hours each morning in the *beis midrash*. In the afternoons, I would take my laptop and settle down in a shady spot near the yeshivah, and do some work for my college courses. To me, this was just about the most perfect spot on earth.

The only problem was that it was en route to the Kotel, so there were often groups of tourists and students walking by. Most of the time, I could ignore the hustle and bustle. But one day, one of the groups that walked by was a particularly noisy, rowdy bunch of teenagers. I ignored them, knowing that within a few minutes, they'd be past me.

But up above me in an apartment building, there was an old woman who apparently could not ignore the noise. She came to her window and looked down to see the cause of the disturbance, but by the time she got there, the teenagers were gone and I was sitting alone in my spot. She concluded that I had been the source of all that noise, and let loose an angry rant directed at me.

I was outraged at being blamed for something that I didn't do and would never have done, but it would have been impossible to get a word in while she was screaming, and I knew that my defense wouldn't have made a difference to her anyway. So I kept my mouth shut and just waited for her to finish and go back to her business.

The next day, the same scene unfolded. The same loud group came by me in a noisy wave while I sat there working peacefully on my laptop. And just as they cleared the area, the woman finally made her way to the window, looked outside and saw me sitting there again. Now, of course, she was sure that I was the cause of all the noise, and she started berating me with even more venom.

At this point, I couldn't just sit there and take this false accusation, so I tried in my pathetic Hebrew to tell her it wasn't me. She didn't even hear me above the sound of her own voice. She just finished her speech and disappeared back into the apartment. I was so frustrated, I felt like marching up to her door and screaming right back at her. But what was the point? I held my peace and went back to work.

You might think that I would have sought out a different spot by now, but suffice it to say that I didn't. On the third day, I gravitated to my favorite shady spot, opened my laptop and began my work. Right on time, the group of teenagers approached from the distance. I could already hear them laughing and shouting. They swarmed past me in their noisy, oblivious way and continued on toward the Kotel. Just as the stragglers were disappearing down the road, the old woman appeared at her window, but this time, she was armed with a water hose.

Without a word, she sent forth a torrent of water onto my head. I bent down over my laptop trying to protect it from harm, but it was ruined. I was drenched from head to toe and humiliated beyond belief. When the water stopped, I turned my face toward her, burning with righteous indignation. I wanted to give her a tongue lashing that she would think about until her last day. I wanted to scream at her that she wasn't fit to live in civilized society. I wanted to, but I held myself back. She shouted some insult down at me, and I simply walked away.

The only place I could think of going in the state I was in was back to the *beis midrash*, back to Aish, where at least my friends would have some pity on me. I knew if I went back there, I could dispel some of the anger I was feeling and restore myself to an even keel.

Of course my entrance into the *beis midrash* raised a lot of eyebrows. I was soaked to the bone, my hair was dripping and my face must have worn an expression of near murderous anger. I told my friends the story, which, from the outside, did have a certain comical aspect to it. So I couldn't blame them for laughing. I laughed with them, but inside, I was still enraged.

But when the laughter petered out, one of my friends said, "Do you know that what happened to you today is straight out of a Gemara that I was just learning?"

I couldn't imagine a Gemara about an angry old lady with a garden hose and a college student with a laptop. "What are you talking about?" I challenged him.

He opened *Maseches Succah* and showed me the Gemara on 52b, which offers this advice: If you meet the *yetzer hara,* drag him into the *beis midrash*, and that is how you will defeat him.

"Look at what you did today," my friend said. "You were about to blow up at this lady and your *yetzer hara* was going to win. Instead, you literally dragged that *yetzer hara* with you into the *beis midrash* to defeat him."

When I saw the wisdom of the Gemara and realized the truth of its words, I was convinced that Hashem was sending me a message to "drag myself and my *yetzer hara* into the *beis midrash*" and devote more of my time to learning. And that is my message to all of you here. We all have different types of *yetzer hara,* but if we drag him into the *beis midrash*, we can defeat him.

By watching and listening for Hashem's messages, we turn the challenges of our lives into productive opportunities for growth. Our setbacks become road-signs pointing the way to our purpose and mission in life.

Chapter 6:

Praying With All Your Heart

Moment of Truth

In the following story, Rabbi Shloime Levenstein relates the power of emunah in Hashem's ability to save us in any situation.

Prior to his weekly Thursday-night *shiur* at the Persian Shul in Bnei Brak, one of Rabbi Yehuda Yosefi's students approached him.

"I have a friend named Benny," he told the Rav. "He just got out of the army, and for the past few weeks, I've been trying to get him to come to the *shiur.* This time, I got him all the way here, but he's sitting in the car refusing to come in. He says he doesn't believe in G-d, so what use would it be to walk into a shul and sit through a *shiur.*

"But since he did come this far, I thought that perhaps if the Rav could go out and speak to him, he might agree to come in."

Rabbi Yosefi was willing to try. He approached the car where Benny was sitting and struck up a friendly conversation. After a few minutes, he said, "You know, I'm going to be giving a *shiur* inside in a couple of minutes. I would love for you to join us."

Benny began shaking his head before the Rav even finished his sentence. "Look, Rabbi, I respect you and I don't mean it as an insult, but I have nothing to gain from a *shiur.* You would first have to convince me that G-d exists for it to make any sense for me to come in."

"You want proof, Benny? I will give you proof," the Rav replied. "You know the story of Moshe Rabbeinu right? Moshe grew up as a prince in Pharaoh's palace. One day he went out to help his fellow Jews and saw an Egyptian beating a Jew. Upon seeing this, Moshe killed the Egyptian.

"Our Rabbis teach us that when Pharaoh found out that Moshe killed an Egyptian, he ordered that Moshe be put to death. Moshe was arrested by Pharaoh's officers and brought to the executioner. However, when he swung the sword at Moshe's neck, a miracle happened. Moshe's neck became as hard as marble and the sword bounced back at the executioner and killed him instead. Moshe was then able to escape the palace of Pharaoh to freedom.

"This story proves another statement made by our Rabbis, which tells us that even when a sharp sword rests on the neck of a man, he should not give up hope of receiving Divine mercy.

"Benny, could there be any explanation for Moshe's life being saved other than the will of Hashem? And if it was Hashem Who saved Moshe, then this proves that there is a Creator of the universe!"

Benny shook his head again. "No, Rabbi, sorry, that's not proof. First of all you have to prove to me that this story with Moshe really happened. Then we can argue about how it happened and who was responsible for it. Why should I simply believe that all these stories are really true?"

Rabbi Yosefi saw that Benny's mind was shut. He answered the misguided man with his own statement of simple faith, which would perhaps accomplish what logic could not. "All the words of our Sages are Torah given to us from heaven, and every word is as true as can be," he said. Then he left the car and returned to the shul to deliver his *shiur.*

Shortly after this encounter, Benny decided to celebrate his freedom by traveling around the world. He had a friend who had gone to Japan, where he had found a business opportunity that was making him a substantial amount of money. The friend had invited Benny to join him, and at this point, that seemed to be the best option. He booked a flight and was soon among some of his fellow Israelis living in Japan.

His first priority was to find a way to support himself while he was there. As a foreigner who didn't speak a word of Japanese, the options were limited, and Benny was soon worrying about how he would sustain himself. Then, his friend offered to help him. "Do you want to make some really good money?" the friend asked. "Sure," Benny answered readily. "Just tell me what I have to do."

The friend launched Benny into a career with the Japanese mafia, and Benny was a model employee. Gradually, he gained the confidence of his bosses and became increasingly involved in their criminal enterprises. As he rose up in the ranks, he began making more money than he had ever thought possible. Somehow he managed to push the violent, criminal underpinnings of his "company" to the back of his mind, and focus on the relatively easy money coming his way. After about a year with the mafia, he was a trusted and successful member of the team.

One day, Benny's boss handed him a suitcase full of money, which was to be brought to a certain location in town. Benny took the suitcase and assured his boss that he would get the job done. But for a few fateful seconds, a chink appeared in Benny's code of blind obedience. Holding the suitcase in his hand as he got into his car, his curiosity began to burn. What was in there, he wondered.

While his mind told him to just do the job, his hands opened the suitcase. Inside, there were perfectly stacked piles of $100 bills. "There must be over $100,000 in here!" he thought. Suddenly, the possibility of breaking out of the mafia and going home to Israel overtook him. He went to the hotel room where he was staying, and called a travel agent to book his ticket. Little did he know that his movements were being followed and his phone was being tapped. His boss' trust only went so far.

A short while after the phone call, there was a sudden knock on the hotel room door. "Housekeeping! Please open the door," a voice called.

"I don't need anything right now," Benny answered.

But the knocking persisted and grew louder. "Why are they

pestering me now?" Benny wondered. Finally, in exasperation, he opened the door to tell them to leave him alone. The moment the door unlatched, three men barged in, grabbed Benny and began beating him. They bound his hands and dragged him out a side door of the hotel into a waiting car.

"Benny, you thought you could run away with our money," one of the men told him. It was the indictment and the conviction, all in one phrase. "Nobody runs away from the mafia."

The men brought Benny to the factory owned by the boss. The cold, calm gaze of the man betrayed no hint of what he was thinking. Yet Benny knew that he had taken a chance that would prove to be fatal.

"We trusted you," said the boss with the tone of a disappointed father. "And you betrayed our trust. Now we have no choice but to kill you."

Benny sat helpless, bound to a chair in the big, isolated factory. Even if he screamed, no one would hear him. There was no way to run, nothing to do.

"Take off his head," the boss ordered one of his men.

The executioner took a large knife out of an ornate box. He began sharpening it with methodical strokes against a special stone. Benny's heart was beating wildly in his chest. He was so filled with fear that he did not know how to contain it. His mind was racing, when suddenly he had a flashback. There he was, sitting in a car with Rabbi Yosefi, listening to what he thought was a fairy tale about Moshe Rabbeinu. He remembered how he was saved from the executioner's sword at the last moment. "Even if a sharp sword is on your neck, don't give up hope in Hashem's salvation," the Rabbi had quoted.

Suddenly Benny screamed out, *"Hashem im Atah kayam, tatzil osi!"* (G-d, if You exist, save me!)

The executioner approached Benny and prepared to kill him. Benny closed his eyes in fear when suddenly, someone shouted, "Stop! Stop! Don't kill him!"

The executioner turned around and saw the boss' wife standing behind him. She screamed at her husband, "You can't kill this man. He saved our son's life!"

The boss signaled for the executioner to drop his sword.

"What are you talking about?" he asked his wife. "When did this man save our son?"

"Remember a few years ago when the earthquake hit Japan?" she said. "Our son was in the street walking home from school. Buildings were shaking and debris was falling. It was terribly dangerous. But this man took him under his wing and walked him home to safety. We owe him so much, and now is the time to repay him for his actions. Please let him go free."

"If that is the case, then you are right," he told his wife. Turning to Benny, he said, "Go back to your country where you belong. I don't want to ever see your face again."

Benny thanked his boss for sparing his life and booked the next flight back to Israel. He could not believe his fortune. He had witnessed the clear intervention of G-d; there was no other possible explanation for what had happened. He had not even been in Japan during that earthquake. G-d had somehow put into this woman's mind the idea that he was the one who had saved her son's life, in order to give Benny the salvation for which he had begged.

Upon returning to Israel, Benny immediately called his friend and told him the entire story of how Hashem had literally saved him when the sword was at his neck, just as Rabbi Yosefi had said. The next Thursday night, Benny was in Bnei Brak, this time inside the shul. He told Rabbi Yosefi that he believed in Hashem and was ready to do *teshuvah*.

> *Rabbi Levenstein explains that besides the emunah in Hashem that this story teaches us, it is also a lesson in emunas chachamim. How did Rabbi Yosefi happen to choose that proof, out of the many other, more easily accepted proofs, to answer Benny's*

doubts? The fact that Rabbi Yosefi chose this specific Chazal about Moshe being saved from the sword shows that Hashem puts the right words into our leaders' mouths to enable them to instruct their people.

In his sefer Derashos HaMaggid, Rav Shabsi Yudelevitch tells a similar story regarding one of his students.

My weekly *shiur* on the *parashah* was attended by a student named Dani. He was a very difficult boy who constantly made a joke of my *shiur,* never seeming to absorb one word in earnest. I tried to reach out to him, but he rejected my efforts. One day, I noticed that he was not present, and for years thereafter, I did not see him. I did, however, hear that he had joined the army.

A few years after Dani disappeared, I noticed a new face at my weekly *shiur*. He was a serious-looking young man with a trimmed black beard. He looked familiar, but I couldn't place him; perhaps he was a relative of another student.

When the *shiur* was over, the young man approached me. "Rebbi, do you remember me?" he asked. "It's Dani."

"Dani?" I repeated in surprise. "So it is! It's good to see you, but I'm sorry, I didn't recognized you."

Opening the gates to what I knew must be a good story, I asked him simply, "So what have you been doing?"

"A lot has happened to me since I used to come to your *shiur*," he answered. "I have been *chozer b'teshuvah* for many years now but Rebbi, I want you to know that I am what I am today because of you."

"Because of me, Dani? What do you mean?"

Then Dani shared his story:

All the words that you used to tell me never went to waste. they were on my heart but I wouldn't let them into my heart, because

I wasn't interested in change, until one fateful day. I had joined the army and became a tank driver. The Yom Kippur War broke out and I was called into battle. I remember that day vividly. We deployed to the front, but when we got there, we found ourselves badly outnumbered. My tank began to take hits and I could not escape to safety. Suddenly, there was a big boom. My tank had taken a direct hit and had burst into flames. I was trapped in an oven. I knew that if I didn't get out within the next few seconds, my life would be over.

A feeling of panic and dread began to overtake me. This was going to be it, the sum total of my life, and what had I done with it? The moments flashed in front of me — all the foolishness and waste. I remembered you, Rebbi, and your *shiurim* that I used to mock. At that moment, I decided that if Hashem got me out of this tank alive, I would do complete *teshuvah*.

The fire spread very rapidly and the heat was choking me, but I screamed out, "Rebbi! Rebbi! I want to do *teshuvah*!"

At that moment, I saw a small clearing in the fire near the door of the tank. The opening was big enough that if I acted quickly I might have a chance. I lunged at the door, opened it, jumped out, and ran from my tank as it exploded into a fireball. When I came out of that tank alive, I knew that I would keep my promise of *teshuvah*. So here I am today, years later, a new person with a new destiny. And it's all thanks to you.

Rav Yudelevitch concludes: Sometimes you teach a student and don't think your words are penetrating. In reality, though, he may not be ready to accept your words, but your lessons and your love are stored in the recesses of his mind. When the time is right, it will make an impact. Rav Shlomo Wolbe would compare this to seeds. Our job is to plant the seeds of chinuch in our children and students and with time and proper nurturing, those seeds will eventually bear fruit.

A High-Flying Prayer

It's easy to underestimate the power of prayer. Saying the same words every day, three times a day, makes mindless repetition a real problem. The cure to that problem is to realize that sincere prayer really works. It can literally alter reality, as these stories illustrate.

"This is the last call for flight 47 to New York," the voice on the loudspeaker announced. "All remaining passengers please board now."

The stragglers who had waited for the last minute to board the plane now quickly gathered up their belongings and rushed to the gate. Off to the side of the waiting area, a young woman stood with face buried in her *siddur*, oblivious to the last call.

"Young lady," a flight attendant called out to her. "You'd better get moving or you'll miss the flight!"

But the young woman didn't respond. It was as if she were encased in a soundproof bubble, just she and Hashem, and nothing else existed. Meanwhile, the flight attendant informed the pilot that there was one passenger who still had not boarded. "She's praying, and it seems that she can't be interrupted," the attendant explained.

The pilot shrugged his shoulders in resignation. What could he do? The girl was praying and he would have to wait. But he would delay takeoff only for a couple of minutes. After all, the airline had a schedule to keep, and the woman certainly could have planned her prayers for earlier in the day. It wasn't his fault if she missed the flight, the pilot reasoned.

The few-minute grace period passed. The pilot looked at his clock; it was getting late. He made his decision to proceed toward takeoff and began his approach to the runway. "We're on our way!" a little boy exclaimed to his father. He pressed his eager face against the window for a good view. Meanwhile, the seasoned travelers read their newspapers or chatted with their seat-mates, trying to relax as they faced the long flight ahead.

Suddenly, the plane came to a halt. "Ladies and gentlemen, we are having some mechanical difficulties," the pilot announced. "Please follow the flight attendants' directions for disembarking; our mechanics will be working on the problem."

A wave of confused muttering rose up in the passenger cabin. People reached for their belongings and began edging their way into the crowded aisles, inching slowly toward the exits. The technical issue was now clear for them all to see and smell; a thick black smoke was billowing out of one engine, surrounding the plane in a menacing cloud.

"How could they put us all into such a junk-heap?" one irate passenger asked out loud.

"Yeah, it looks like it's about to blow up," another concurred.

The entire grumbling, frustrated crowd reassembled in the waiting area and looked for ways to pass the time while a crew of mechanics scrutinized the engine part by part, seeking the source of the smoke. There did not seem to be anything amiss. In fact, the smoke disappeared as quickly and mysteriously as it had appeared. Once the mechanics were satisfied that there were no hidden problems, they gave the go-ahead to resume the flight.

Once again, a voice on the loudspeaker urged the passengers to board the plane and prepare for take-off. Rabbi Chaim Zeyid, the head of Yeshivas Toras Yosef of Bnei Brak, was among those getting ready to board. In addition to running a yeshivah, he was involved in Arachim, a *kiruv* organization in Israel, and was on his way to America for a fundraising trip.

Before the passengers had finished boarding the first time, Rabbi Zeyid had taken note of the young woman who opted to miss her flight rather than interrupt her prayers. Now, he noticed that she was still in the waiting area, but she was heading away from the gate rather than taking the opportunity to catch her flight. Perhaps she didn't even realize that this was the same flight she had been scheduled to take.

He dashed quickly in her direction, trying to catch her before she wandered too far. "Excuse me! Excuse me!" he called.

The young woman turned around and saw Rabbi Zeyid approaching.

"I'm Rabbi Zeyid," he said. "I noticed that, earlier, you were davening while the flight was boarding, and you missed the final call. I just want you to know that the flight was delayed and everyone had to get off the plane. They're boarding again right now, so you can actually catch the flight!"

"Fantastic!" the girl replied. She and Rabbi Zeyid both hastened to the gate in time to board.

Once the plane was finally airborne, a flight attendant named Uri approached Rabbi Zeyid.

"What do you make of all the strange events that happened today with this flight?" he asked.

"Honestly, I thought about it and realized that the only possible answer is that there was tremendous *hashgachah pratis* (Divine intervention) here today. You and I both know that this type of thing never happens. Today, though, this young woman's prayers were so powerful that I believe she elicited Hashem's help. He wanted to make sure that she wouldn't miss the flight, so He caused the engine to spew smoke."

Uri nodded in agreement. "Rabbi, you know I am not a religous Jew, but I couldn't help but come to the same conclusion. I saw how that woman prayed with such devotion and it seems that her prayers literally stopped the plane in its tracks."

Seizing upon Uri's moment of inspiration, Rabbi Zeyid suggested that he attend a seminar offered by Arachim, the *kiruv* organization he was involved in. "You could learn a little more about Judaism," the rabbi suggested. "You might even learn how to use the power of prayer that you just saw displayed."

Only a few days later, Uri attended his first Arachim seminar. Intrigued and inspired, he began attending every week. Within just a few months, he had become a *baal teshuvah,* fully embracing a life of Torah and mitzvos.

Six months later, Rabbi Zeyid got a phone call from Uri.

"Someone has suggested a *shidduch* for me," he explained. "Would you be willing to look into the girl's references for me?"

Rabbi Zeyid was delighted to help Uri ascend to the next stage in his life. He began making phone calls to the young lady's references and discovering that she was indeed someone of very fine character and a high level of *emunah.* He heard from several references that in recent months, she had taken upon herself a special commitment to *tefillah* as a *zechus* for finding her long-awaited *shidduch.* On one particular call, the young lady's close friend illustrated the point with a story.

"She has an amazing power of *tefillah,*" the friend said. "I mean, really unusual. In fact, recently she was waiting for a plane from Tel Aviv to New York and she was in the middle of davening Minchah while they were boarding. She just stood there and finished davening even though she would miss the flight. In the end — such *hashgachah pratis* — the plane was delayed by a strange mechanical problem, and she got on after all."

Rabbi Zeyid thanked the friend and quickly dialed Uri's number. "You've found your *bashert!*" he exclaimed. And indeed, he had.

This young woman's heartfelt tefillos *stopped a plane, brought a non-religious man back to his roots, and miraculously brought about her long-awaited* shidduch. *That's what one would call a high-flying prayer.*

The story reminds me of a different mysterious plane flight that was miraculously affected by a prayer

Among the many highly dedicated students at Yeshiva Ponovezh in Bnei Brak, Moshe Gertner stood out. Not only did he learn with enormous concentration, not only did he scrupulously use every available moment for learning, but in addition, never once did he miss the *mussar shiur* given each week by the *Mashgiach*, Rav Yechezkel Levenstein.

Every Wednesday night at 7, without fail, Moshe was in his seat, pen and notebook in hand, ready to soak up the *Mashgiach's* inspiring words. If he had a wedding to attend, he would go after the *shiur.* If he needed to take care of any personal business, he would make sure to schedule it for some other block of time. Everyone in the yeshivah knew that nothing would keep Moshe from the *shiur.*

Then, Moshe got engaged. Even with all the preparations and events surrounding the happy occasion, he still made sure to maintain his 100 percent attendance. Even his wedding was scheduled on a Thursday night so as not to throw him off course. However, when his mother scheduled a flight from New York to arrive in Tel Aviv the night before the wedding, Wednesday at 7, Moshe finally faced a scheduling conflict that was not so simple to brush aside.

The idea of missing the *shiur* seemed to Moshe untenable. On the other hand, failing to greet his mother at the airport would be even worse. Was there no way to do both? Moshe brought his concern to the *Mashgiach*, who confirmed that his first obligation was to honor his mother.

That night, when Moshe davened Maariv, he begged Hashem to help him to somehow be able to meet his mother without missing the *shiur*. An idea occurred to him; perhaps the plane would come early, and he would have time to get back to yeshivah by 7.

It seemed like a long, long shot, but on the designated Wednesday, the day before Moshe's wedding, he arrived at the airport at 5 p.m., two hours early. Shortly after he arrived, there was an announcement: the flight from New York was arriving at its gate. Soon he saw his mother emerging from customs.

"How did you know we were coming in early?" she asked.

"I just had a feeling," he replied in all honesty.

As the mother and son headed out toward the airport exit among the crowd of travelers, they spotted the pilot of the flight. Unable to contain his amazement, Moshe approached him and asked, "How did the flight get here so early?"

"I really don't know," the pilot answered. "In 27 years of flying, I've never seen anything like it. We had this unbelievable tail-wind that pushed us along the entire way. I've been a half-hour early, even an hour early. But two hours early? Never!"

The pilot couldn't explain it, but Moshe knew the truth. Hashem had heard his prayer and rearranged the world so that he could attend the *Mashgiach's* shiur. Moshe would later comment that, grateful as he was for this quiet miracle, it was all in a day's work for Hashem.

"If Hashem could split the sea, couldn't He arrange that an airplane should arrive 2 hours early so that a *talmid* could attend his rebbi's *shiur*?"

Indeed, no request is too difficult when it's riding on the wings of a prayer.

BREAKTHROUGH

What are the ingredients for the successful chinuch of children? Certainly one needs to send his child to a good yeshivah and be involved in the child's studies. However, the first and most important ingredient for a child's success is his parents' davening for siyata d'Shmaya, coupled, if possible, with the child's own tefillos. This is the strategy that works, even when all else fails.

As Rabbi Fried* read the Gemara with his class, he noticed that Dovi's eyes were fixated on a spot near the window. Maybe there was a bug climbing up the wall, or perhaps the boy's eyes were simply gazing at a blank spot while his mind wandered to more exciting venues. Ruefully, the rebbi interrupted his student's reverie to bring him back to reality.

"Dovi, please find the place," said Rabbi Fried. Dovi, caught off-guard as always, turned his eyes to the *sefer* in front of him and moved his finger along the lines as if trying to resume where he had left off. Sadly, he did not even know where the lesson had begun, let alone what the class was reviewing at the moment.

Dovi's problem was not a lack of motivation. The other boys in the class seemed to be so engaged in the learning. The Rebbi seemed to really enjoy the questions they asked and the answers they offered. They were all "on the same page," while Dovi was not even in the same book. He longed to be part of the give and take, the excitement and camaraderie of the class. He tried with all his might to focus and understand, but he might as well have been reading Chinese. His parents willingly hired tutor after tutor to help him, but to no avail.

With his self-esteem so critically wounded, Dovi began to shrink away from the other boys in class. He rarely went outdoors for recess, fearing that no one would want to play with a loser. Eventually, he slid so completely into the role of the outsider that the other students began seeing him in that light. He heard them laugh when the rebbi would call on him and find him, as always, completely lost. They mimicked his vacant stare and his mumbled replies. Dovi began to hate school.

One morning, Dovi could not find the strength to get out of bed and face another day. "I can't do it any more, Mommy," he cried. "I try as hard as I can. When will I ever feel like a normal kid?"

"Come on, Dovi," his mother gently prodded. "You'll see, things are going to get better. Just keep doing the best you can, and Hashem will help you. You have to keep trying, even though it's hard." She said these words with as much conviction as she could muster, but inside her head, other words were ringing out: "You poor, poor child! What will ever be with you?" She held back her tears of pity as she urged her son off to school each morning, knowing that he faced a daily encounter with pure misery.

One day, Dovi came into class with a bit more bounce in his step than usual. He sat down, opened his Gemara and began following the words the rebbi was reviewing. "Wait a minute," he thought to himself. "This doesn't seem to make sense!" His arm flew up in the air and his rebbi called on him. Dovi asked the first cogent question he had asked all year.

Rabbi Fried was startled by Dovi's sudden involvement in the learning. He answered the question, ending his explanation by saying, "and that settles the issue."

"But Rebbi, it seems that we are still left with a question," Dovi responded. As he explained his reasoning, Rabbi Fried marveled at the brilliance his student was exhibiting. "I wonder what's going on," the rebbi thought. "I wonder how long it will last."

On the following day, not only did Dovi ask more insightful questions, but he read the Gemara with fluency and explained its logic with crystal clarity. By now, the other boys in the class were observing Dovi with fascinated awe. What happened to the old Dovi? How did he become such a genius? They, too, imagined that it was some kind of fluke or trick whose source would soon be revealed. Yet day after day, Dovi continued to perform, eventually outperforming the brightest boys in the class.

The mystery of Dovi's 180-degree turnaround preoccupied Rabbi Fried's mind. How could such a change occur? He decided to call Dovi's mother and inquire: there had to be some new learning system or tutor or motivator that had come on the scene and opened Dovi's mind.

"I'm sure you've noticed that Dovi's most recent test grades are light-years ahead of what he's been doing up until now. And I want you to know that his participation in class is also on a very high level," Rabbi Fried told Dovi's mother. "I can't help wandering what you have been doing to help him, because whatever it is, I've never seen anything work so well and so fast."

"Baruch Hashem! Baruch Hashem!" Dovi's mother exulted. "It's so good to hear this report! You are right that I've been doing something to help him ... I've been davening, and so has he!" She then told this story:

This year has been Dovi's hardest since he started *cheder*, because he just did not have the skills to begin Gemara. Each day when he came home from school, he walked through the door looking so sad and defeated. He would tell me how everyone else in class seemed to understand what was going on, and he would cry to me and ask, "Why am I so dumb?" My heart broke for my little Dovi, and then it struck me that perhaps there was something I could do.

I had tried every practical way to help Dovi, but I had forgotten the most basic step, to daven for his success. I decided that the best time to daven for him would be when I *bentch licht* Friday evening, which is an opportune time to pray for children's success in Torah study.

So one Friday afternoon, after I set up the candles, I called Dovi over and told him, "I want you to stand here with me near the candles while I daven for your success. And I want you to daven for your success as well. Perhaps our *tefillos* combined will bring Hashem's help, and your heart will open to your Torah learning."

I lit the candles and covered my eyes, and as I started to daven for my son, my heart was flooded with so much emotion. I was overcome by his pain, by my pity for his situation and my fears of what could become of him if things didn't change. Tears came to my eyes, but soon, I was not just teary-eyed, but crying. Dovi stood next to me, and when he heard me crying, his heart broke open too. Both of us stood there crying and praying and knocking down the gates of Heaven. We have been doing this week after week, with all of our hearts, and from what you are telling me now, Rabbi Fried, our *tefillos* are being answered!

In the simple story of this compassionate mother, Rabbi Fried saw illustrated a truth he had always known. A mother's tears and prayers can penetrate any wall, break down any barrier, and rally the power of Heaven to the cause of her precious child.

While we all must do the best we can to help our children in their learning, only Hashem can crown our hishtadlus with success. Ultimately, our tefillos are the hishtadlus that counts the most.

A Buried Treasure

A prayer that comes from the depths of one's heart is similar to a buried treasure. Its value is priceless, but it first must be uncovered.

The news spread fast throughout Eretz Yisrael. It seemed outrageous that in 2008, Jews would still have to be fighting vandalism and destruction of their cemeteries around the world. But that was the case. The city of Grodna in Belarus was building a sports stadium, and in the course of construction, Jewish graves had been disturbed and now, Jewish bones were lying in large storage containers in the basement of a city building.

Rabbi Dovid Shmidel, head of the Asra Kadisha, swung into action trying to remedy the situation. His organization had been formed to save Jewish cemeteries, and where that was not possible, to bring the desecrated bones to a proper Jewish reburial. Certainly, storage containers in a basement did not qualify as a proper burial.

His first step was to contact rabbanim and government officials with whom he had worked on matters within Russia. He pursued that course until he was able to get permission to have someone come to Grodno and bury the bones properly. Yaakov Waller* was the agent he called upon to accomplish this holy task.

Yaakov booked a flight from Israel to Belarus. He was told that he should do his utmost to bury the bones before nightfall of the day he arrives, as according to halachah the optimal time for burial is on the same day as death. In this case, although the time of death was long ago, the unearthed bones constituted a disgrace to the dead, and the quicker they were buried, the better.

On arrival in Grodno, Yaakov quickly found the Jewish cemetery. He told the person who manned the office that he had been sent from Israel in order to properly rebury the bones that had been unearthed.

"I am sorry, but the person in charge of that department is not here right now," the man told him. Yaakov said he would wait.

"But he will not be back soon," said the man. "He is on a two-week vacation."

Yaakov was not deterred. "That's all right," he said. "I will stay here until he comes back. I have plenty of food in my suitcase."

When the official saw that Yaakov was not going to budge, he got to work. He made a few phone calls and finally told Yaakov, "Go to the large building across the street and the guard will lead you to the basement, where you will find the crates of bones that you are looking for."

Once Yaakov located the bones, he went outside and hired a man to help him load the crates into his rental van. He would then drive them to the location where they were to be reburied. He explained to the worker that it was very important that they get the job done before sundown, and he would pay him extra to work fast.

After loading the van, they returned to the Jewish cemetery and unloaded the boxes. By this time, Yaakov saw that the hour had gotten late. "We have to really work fast if we want to get this done before sunset," Yaakov told the worker. "We have about an hour."

The worker replied, "Are you joking, Rabbi? There is no way to get this done before sunset. Do you see how large these crates are? Even if we got two more workers, it would take us hours to dig up the ground in time. You would need 50 people in order to do all this within an hour!"

Yaakov realized that his worker was right. There was no way it would be possible to get it done in time. Besides the obstacle of time, Yaakov's energy was spent. He had traveled for hours on a plane, and he was tired and hungry. He had rushed to load the bones into his car and get to the cemetery in time, and now he couldn't even get the job done right.

He looked up to heaven and said, "*Ribono Shel Olam,* I did all that I could for Your honor. I flew in from Eretz Yisrael. I struggled to get a hold of the bones, I dragged them out here together with a worker. I wanted to get it done today but what more can I do? You have to take care of the rest."

He did not yet finish offering his heartfelt prayer when someone tapped him on the shoulder from behind. Yaakov turned around and was shocked to see a yeshivah *bachur* standing before him.

"We are looking for a certain *kever* here," the *bachur* said. "Are you able to help us out?"

"Who is 'we'?" asked Yaakov.

The *bachur* turned around and pointed to a bus in the distance filled with more *bachurim*.

"How many *bachurim* are in that bus?" asked Yaakov.

"We are a group of 50 boys," the *bachur* replied. "Our yeshiva came from America, and we are here visiting various graves of *tzaddikim*. We happened to be in Grodno, so we figured we would daven at some *kevarim* here. Do you think you could show us around?"

Yaakov could not believe what was unfolding before his eyes. He said, "Before I help you out, I have a big mitzvah that I need you to help me with. Do you mind if I come to your bus and talk to the boys?"

Yaakov boarded the bus and told the bachurim why he had traveled from Eretz Yisrael. He had a mission — to show respect for the dead — and there was no way he could fulfill his job unless he got a lot of help digging and burying the bones so that it could be done before sunset.

"I am not a miracle worker, but all I know is that I davened for Hashem to help me and while I was davening, you all appeared. I believe heaven wants us to do this today. Otherwise we would have never met up."

The *bachurim* heard the call and immediately got to work. With shovels in their hands, they began to dig and within the hour, all the bones were buried. The sun hovered just over the horizon. They made a *minyan* to daven Minchah and Yaakov thanked Hashem from the bottom of his heart for helping him do the impossible.

When Yaakov got home, he reported to Rav Shmidel that his mission was accomplished.

But the story though doesn't end there.

On his return to his house in Bnei Brak, Yaakov was still very moved by the way Hashem had so clearly heard his prayers. In fact, he had never before received an answer as soon as the prayer left his lips, even though he had prayed for many things in his life.

In fact, for the past few years, he had been praying for his daughters to find *shidduchim,* and that prayer was not yet answered. Yaakov looked up to heaven and from the depths of his heart, he offered another prayer:

"*Ribono Shel Olam,* You gave me the merit to perform a great mitzvah, but my happiness is not complete since in my home one of my daughters is 31 and not married and my other daughter is 35 and not married. Please, Hashem, I beg of You, let them find their *zivug* soon and begin life in their new home with complete joy."

Within two months, both of his daughters were engaged. When Yaakov told this story to a *talmid chacham* he explained, "When you do *chesed* for Hashem, then Hashem does *chesed* for you."

In this story, Yaakov did not merely daven that Hashem should miraculously bury the bones, but rather he exerted himself to the best of his abilities. Yaakov showed Hashem that he really believed that He could finish the job for him, and then He did.

And that reminds me of a sweet story I heard recently.

There was a *Mashgiach* in Eretz Yisrael who, upon the birth of every great-grandchild, would buy the child an outfit. For the boys he would buy a blue outfit and for the girls he would buy pink. One of his granddaughters did not have any children after many years of marriage. Finally, after all that time, she gave birth to a baby girl. Now she would have her long-awaited turn to receive her grandfather's baby gift.

The day came when her grandfather arrived at her house carrying a small suitcase. Inside it, there were six pink outfits.

The granddaughter was bewildered. "*Zeide*, I only had one baby. Why did you bring me six outfits?"

The *Mashgiach* explained. "Do you know when I buy these outfits? Every year when I travel to America on behalf of the yeshivah, I call Bubby and ask her who is awaiting a *simchah*. She tells me who is expecting a child and I buy an outfit for them. Every single year I went out and bought an outfit for you, because I said to myself, if I really believed that my prayers would be answered, I would have to show it by buying a baby outfit for you."

"*Zeide*, that means that you have been carrying in your bag six outfits for me all this time?"

The *Mashgiach* answered, "Not six! I am carrying twelve outfits because I didn't know if you would have a boy or a girl."

There was a young married man who had not yet had a child. For several years, he davened to be blessed with a baby, but the answer he was hoping for didn't come. He decided that perhaps he wasn't davening hard enough, and so his *Shemoneh Esrei* grew longer and longer.

One day, his friend called him up and told him that he was cleaning out his garage and had some items in good condition that he wanted to give away.

"Why don't you come by and take a look. Take anything you want," the friend said.

"The young man went to his friend's garage, and standing in the corner, he saw a beautiful baby stroller. He picked it up and asked his friend, "Can I have this?"

The friend said, "Sure you can. Take whatever you want."

As the young man left with the baby stroller, he thought, "Here I am praying every day for a baby. If I really believe that Hashem will answer me, I should take this stroller home and be ready for the baby."

That year, his wife gave birth to twin boys. Yes ... it was a double stroller.

I conclude with a letter that Rav Shimshon Pincus once wrote to a struggling bachur, teaching him that when we daven, we have to make our conversation with Hashem real.

Dear Yossi:

I have read your letter, and I don't feel that I am on the level to give you eitzos (advice) on what you should do in this situation. However, I will tell you what my humble opinion is. I understand from your letter that you are doing your best to grow in Torah and yiras Shamayim, and so I believe that you have done proper hishtadlus (effort) already. Now, though, I believe you have reached a point in your life where you are going to need some outside help to get you to where you have to go. This is because to grow in Torah and to have a desire to learn is not a simple feat and you need someone to help lead you on the road to success.

I am enclosing the name and address of someone who can certainly help you solve all your problems. Please send your request to him.

They call Him "Hashem."

He is very strong. As we know, He created the entire world. And I know for a fact that He loves you as well, and is waiting for you to turn to Him for assistance.

It will not be difficult at all for you to find His address, because He is found in every place in the world. Even during this moment when you are reading this letter, you are able to turn to Him.

I am writing this to you because many people think that tefillah is about performing a mitzvah or reaching a high level. Although that is true, it is not the main thing. The main thing about tefillah is recognizing that Hashem is "chai vekayam" (alive and exists) — that you can make a personal relationship with Him, and He will never forsake one who does so! And know that the more practical and simple the thing you need, the better off you will be. Talk to Hashem about the problems facing you, and keep on asking Hashem to help you until He answers your prayer.

Forget about seeking out help elsewhere. Go to the One Who can truthfully help you solve your problems. Grab onto Him and never let go, until you have attained all of your heart's desires.

All the best,
Shimshon Dovid Pincus

Rav Pincus taught Yossi that Hashem is real and relevant. You don't have to look far for help; you simply have to look up.

GLOSSARY

GLOSSARY

achakeh lo b'chol yom sheyavo, v'af al pi sheyismame'ah im kol zeh achakeh lo — "I anticipate him [the messiah] every day; even though he may delay, nevertheless I anticipate him." a popular song based on one of the 13 fundamental principles of faith.

achdus — unity

ahavas chesed — love of doing kindness

ahavas haTorah — love of Torah

ahavas Yisrael — love of Jews

aliyah — being called to the Torah

Amen yehei Sh'mei rabba — "Amen, may His great Name [be blessed forever and ever],"a primary communal response in the Kaddish prayer.

aron kodesh — holy ark in the synagogue, where the Torah Scrolls are kept

ashreinu ma tov chelkeinu — we are fortunate, how good is our portion

aufruf — being called to the Torah on the week before one's wedding

Av haRachamim — Merciful Father (referring to G-d)

avodas Hashem — service of G-d

baal tokei'a — the one who blows the shofar on Rosh Hashanah

baal teshuvah (pl., *baalei teshuvah;* fem., *baalas teshuvah, baalos teshuvah)* — one who has chosen to become Torah observant

bachur — a boy; a young man

baruch atah Hashem, Elokeinu melech haolam, shehakol nih'yeh bidvaro — "Blessed are You, Hashem, our G-d, King of the universe, through whose word everything came to be"; the blessing recited over foods that do not have another, more specific, blessing

baruch Hashem — thank G-d

bas melech — daughter of the king

Bava Metzia — a tractate of the Talmud

bechal levavcha — with all your heart

beged — garment

beis midrash (pl. *batei midrash)* — study hall

bekishe — the long coat worn by chassidim

ben Torah — one who leads a Torah life

bentch licht — candle lighting

bentching — (Yiddish) blessing, esp. grace after meals
berachah — blessing
berachah acharonah — blessing recited after eating
bikur cholim — visiting the sick
bimah — table in synagogue on which the Torah is placed to be read
bimheirah veyameinu — speedily, in our days
bircas Kohanim — the Priestly Blessing, recited during the *chazzan's* repetition of the *Shemoneh Esrei*
bris milah — circumcision
chai vekayam — alive and exists
chareidi, (pl. *chareidim)* — one who is scrupulously observant
chazzan — leader of the prayer service
cheder — school
cheirem — excommunication
chesed — kindness
chiddush — novel Torah thought
chiloni — irreligious person
chinuch — education
chizuk — encourgament; strengthening
chozer b'teshuvah — one who has "returned," i.e. has become religiously observant
chumash; (pl. *chumashim)* — a volume containing the five books of the Torah; the book of the Torah
chuppah — wedding canopy; the wedding ceremony
dati — religiously observant
derashah — sermon
divrei Torah — Torah thoughts
eis ratzon — a propitious time
eitzos — advice
emunah — faith
eruv — a halachic enclosure that allows one to carry outside on the Sabbath
es ist ein Gotteskleid — (German) "it is a religious garment"
esrog — citron, taken as one of the Four Species during the Succos Festival
frum — Torah-observant
*gadol (*pl. *gedolim)* — an adult; a Torah leader
gadol hador — Torah leader of the generation
geulah — redemption
gezel akum — items stolen from a non-Jew
ha'adamah — (lit.: from the earth) the blessing made on foods that grow from the ground
hachnasas orchim — hosting guests
Hakadosh Baruch Hu — the Holy One, blessed is He
hakol — everything
halachah (pl. *halachos)* — Jewish law and practice
Hallel — payer of praise and thanksgiving recited on Festivals
harbatzas haTorah — spreading Torah
Hashem echad u'Shemo echad — G-d is One and His Name is One
hashgachah — supervision
hashgachah pratis — Divine providence

hasmadah baTorah — diligence in Torah study
hatzlachah — success
hishtadlus — effort
iy"H — if G-d wills it
Kaddish — prayer sanctifying G-d's name, often recited by mourners
kallah — bride
kavanah — concentration
kedushah. — sanctity
kehillah — community
kesubah — marriage document
kever — grave
kiddush Hashem — sanctification of G-d's name
kiruv — (lit.: bringing near) outreach to teach people about their Jewish heritage
kol tuv — all that is good
kollel — academy of higher Jewish learning, whose students are mostly married men
korban pesach — the Passover offering
ksav mechilah — a letter of forgiveness
kvatter — the one who carries the baby in for the bris
lashon hara — evil speech, slander
leichter — candelabra
lev Yehudi — a Jewish heart
levayah — funeral
limud haTorah — Torah study
lulav — palm frond, taken as one of the Four Species during the Succos Festival
maasim tovim — good deeds
malach, (pl. *malachim)* — angel
mashgiach — spiritual mentor in a yeshivah; kashruth supervisor
mashiach tzidkeinu — the righteous messiah
masok mi'devash — sweeter than honey
mechutzaf — an insolent person
middos — character traits
mikveh — ritual bath
minyan — a prayer quorum
mishpachah — family
mispalel (pl. *mispalelim)* — one who prays
mohel — one who performs a circumcision
mussar — ethical teachings
nachas — satisfaction, enjoyment
neshamah — soul
nisayon — challenge
nishmas kol chai — (lit.: the soul of all living things) a prayer of praise and thanksgiving to G-d, that begins with these words
nivul peh — obscenity
od paam — again
oleh chadash — a new immigrant to Israel
oneg Shabbos — informal get-together in honor of the Sabbath
parnassah — sustenance, livelihood
peyos — sidelocks
pirchei — a youth group for young boys
posek hador — the leading halachic authority of the generation
rabbosai — my teachers; a form of address
refuah — remedy
Ribono shel Olam — Master of the universe; i.e., G-d
ruach — spirit

ruck — frock
sandek — one who holds the baby during the circumcision
seder — the formal meal on the first nights of Passover ; a study period session
*sefer (*pl. *sefarim)* — book, esp. on a Torah topic
segulah — spiritual remedy
seudah — meal
seudas hodaah — a meal to express gratitude to G-d
shailos — questions, esp. halachic questions
shaliach — messenger; representative
shalom aleichem — (lit.: peace unto you) a greeting; a Sabbath song that begins with those words
Shechinah — the Divine Presence
sheish mitzvos temidios — the six constant mitzvos that apply and can be performed by every person at all times
sheker — falsehood
Shema Yisrael — the Jews' declaration of faith
shemiras halashon — guarding one's speech
Shemoneh Esrei — the prayer containing 18 blessings, recited three times a day
shiur — lecture; class; requisite measure
shivah — the seven-day mourning period for a relative
shomer Shabbos — Sabbath observant
shtetl — a small Europen village
shtiebel — a small synagogue
shtreimel — the fur hat worn by chassidic Jews
siddur (pl *siddurim*) — prayer book
simchah — joy; festive celebration
siyata d'Shmaya — Divine assistance
siyum — completion of a tractate of the Talmud; the celebration of this achievement
tallis — prayer shawl
*talmid (*pl: *talmidim)* — disciple
talmid chacham — a Torah scholar
tashlich — a prayer recited during High Holy Day season, usually at a body of water, during which we symbolically cast away our sins
*tefillah (*pl. *tefillos)* — prayer
tefillin — phylacteries, leather boxes containing select Torah verses, worn by men on the arm and on the head
tefillin shel rosh — the head-tefillin
tefillin shel yad — the arm-tefillin
Tehillim — Psalms
teshuvah — repentance
tov meod — very good
tzaddik (pl. *tzaddikim)* — a righteous person
tzedakah — charity
tzenius — modesty
vetaher libeinu — and purify our hearts [to serve You in truth]; a popular song that includes those words
yehi zichro baruch — may his memory be a blessing
yetzer hara — the evil inclination
Yiddishkeit — Judaism
yiras Shamayim — fear of Heaven

yizkor — the memorial prayer recited on Festivals
z'man — time; a semester
zechus — merit, privilege
zechusim — merits
zeide — (Yiddish) grandfather
zemiros — songs, esp. those sung at Sabbath and Festival meals
zivug — marriage partner
zuto shel yam — property that was carried away by a tide, which may be kept by the finder

This volume is part of
THE ARTSCROLL SERIES®
an ongoing project of
translations, commentaries and expositions on
Scripture, Mishnah, Talmud, Midrash, Halachah,
liturgy, history, the classic Rabbinic writings,
biographies and thought.

For a brochure of current publications
visit your local Hebrew bookseller
or contact the publisher:

Mesorah Publications, ltd
4401 Second Avenue
Brooklyn, New York 11232
(718) 921-9000
www.artscroll.com